THE
WISDOM
LITERATURE

GENERAL EDITORS

Gene M. Tucker, *Old Testament*

Charles B. Cousar, *New Testament*

INTERPRETING
I · B · T
BIBLICAL TEXTS

THE
WISDOM
LITERATURE

Richard J. Clifford

ABINGDON PRESS
Nashville

THE WISDOM LITERATURE

Copyright © 1998 by Abingdon Press

This book is printed on acid-free, recycled, elemental-chlorine-free paper.

Library of Congress Cataloging-in-Publication Data

Clifford, Richard J.
  The Wisdom literature / Richard J. Clifford.
    p.   cm. — (Interpreting Biblical texts)
  Includes bibliographical references and index.
  ISBN 0-687-00846-8 (pbk: alk. paper)
    1. Wisdom literature—Criticism, interpretation, etc.   I. Title.
  II. Series.
  BS1455.C58   1998
  223'.06—dc21   98-13825
                                                                              CIP

ISBN 13: 978-0-687-00846-9

Scripture quotations, except where noted, are from the New Revised Standard Version Bible, copyright © 1989, by the Division of Christian Education of the National Council of the Churches of Christ in the United States of America. Used by permission.

For use of *ANET,* Pritchard, J.B., ed., *Ancient Near Eastern Texts Relating to the Old Testament.* Copyright © 1969 by Princeton University Press. Reprinted by permission of Princeton University Press.

08   09   10   11   12   13   14   15   16   17   —   15   14   13   12   11

MANUFACTURED IN THE UNITED STATES OF AMERICA

To
Frederick L. Moriarty, S.J.

My First Teacher of the Bible
and of Hebrew

CONTENTS

FOREWORD

Biblical texts create worlds of meaning, and invite readers to enter them. When readers enter such textual worlds, which are often strange and complex, they are confronted with theological claims. With this in mind, the purpose of this series is to help serious readers in their experience of reading and interpreting, to provide guides for their journeys into textual worlds. The controlling perspective is expressed in the operative word of the title—*interpreting*. The primary focus of the series is not so much on the world *behind* the texts or out of which the texts have arisen (though these worlds are not irrelevant) as on the world *created by* the texts in their engagement with readers.

Each volume addresses two questions. First, what are the critical issues of interpretation that have emerged in the recent history of scholarship and to which serious readers of the texts need to be sensitive? Some of the concerns of scholars are interesting and significant, but frankly peripheral to the interpretative task. Others are more central. How they are addressed influences decisions readers make in the process of interpretation. Thus the authors call attention to these basic issues and indicate their significance for interpretation.

Second, in struggling with particular passages or sections of material, how can readers be kept aware of the larger world created by the text as a whole? How can they both see the forest and examine individual trees? How can students encountering the story of David and Bathsheba in 2 Samuel 11 read it in light of its context in the larger story, the Deuteronomistic History that includes the books of Deuteronomy through 2 Kings? How can readers of Galatians fit what they learn into the theological coherence and polarities of the larger perspective drawn from all the letters of Paul? Thus each volume provides an overview of the literature as a whole.

The aim of the series is clearly pedagogical. The authors offer their own understanding of the issues and texts, but are more concerned about guiding the reader than engaging in debates with other scholars. The series is meant to serve as a resource, alongside other resources such as commentaries and specialized studies, to aid students in the exciting and often risky venture of interpreting biblical texts.

Gene M. Tucker
General Editor, *Old Testament*

Charles B. Cousar
General Editor, *New Testament*

PREFACE

The series Interpreting Biblical Texts aims to introduce the reader to the world of the text. That aim makes this book different from other books on biblical wisdom literature. Thus, unlike the admirable introduction of Roland Murphy, *The Tree of Life: An Exploration of Biblical Wisdom Literature*, or that of James Crenshaw, *Old Testament Wisdom: An Introduction*, this book is not a series of essays about the wisdom books and their forms and ideas. Our book gives just enough information to make you a good reader. The series in which this book appears assumes that the most important thing one can do is engage the sacred text.

What is "just enough information to make you a good reader"? It varies for each of the wisdom books. Hence each chapter of this book is different. For Proverbs, for example, one needs to understand the genres (instruction and saying) and how they work in the book and the metaphorical dimension. Job and Wisdom of Solomon are quite different, for their structure is important to the meaning. Readers need to be guided step-by-step through the whole and follow the argument. Qoheleth (Ecclesiastes) is unique; in one sense its observations are disjointed, but in another sense they are the reflections of a single personality looking at life from several perspectives. One must therefore attend to the unity and structure while allowing for randomness and surprise. To comprehend Sirach, one needs to be aware of its design, doctrines, and development of traditional motifs and ideas. The Song of Songs demands a knowledge of the world of its symbols and motifs, as well as a sense of the exchange between the lovers. The following chapters, each with a slightly different method, aim to form a sensitive and interested reader of each book in the wisdom library.

PREFACE

The chief task belongs to the reader, however—reading the biblical wisdom literature yourself. Other people's summaries and assessments are no substitute. Let me end with three practical hints.

1) Use a good translation. Sometimes it is useful to look at a second translation, but base your study on one text. Translations of the wisdom literature vary in quality. Among the best translations of the wisdom literature are *Tanakh*, the Jewish Publication Society version, and the *New American Bible*. For Job, the best translations are found in the commentaries of N. Habel and M. Pope, in that order.

2) At this stage, it is better not to use the large commentaries except for problematic or fundamental passages. More useful are this book and the brief introductions and notes of modern annotated Bibles. Read and reread the biblical text, penciling in your own annotations if that is helpful. For problems, the large commentaries are always there, but most of the literature is accessible with a little work. What you puzzle out yourself will always be yours.

3) It is good to remember that great literature expresses its own time well and yet is perennially true. By a wonderful paradox, we understand what is perennially true and touching in the act of appreciating the difference and the distance between ourselves and the text.

ABBREVIATIONS

AEL   M. Lichtheim, *Ancient Egyptian Literature* (Berkeley: University of California Press, 1975–80). 3 vols.

ANET   *Ancient Near Eastern Texts Relating to the Old Testament* (ed. J. B. Pritchard; 3rd ed.; Princeton, N.J.: Princeton University Press, 1969)

BM   *Before the Muses: An Anthology of Akkadian Literature* (Bethesda, Md.: CDL, 1993). 2 vols.

BTB   *Biblical Theology Bulletin*

BWL   G. Lambert, *Babylonian Wisdom Literature* (Oxford: Clarendon, 1960)

CBQ   *Catholic Biblical Quarterly*

CBQMS   Catholic Biblical Quarterly—Monograph Series

EV   English Version

HTS   Harvard Theological Studies

JAOS   Journal of the American Oriental Society

JBL   Journal of Biblical Literature

JSOTSup Journal for the Study of the Old Testament—Supplement Series

KTU   M. Dietrich et al., eds. *The Cuneiform Alphabetic Texts from Ugarit, Ras Ibn Han: and Other Places* KTU: 2nd enlarged ed. (Münster: Ugarit-Verlag, 1995)

MFM   Dalley, *Myths from Mesopotamia: Creation, the Flood, Gilgamesh and Others* (Oxford: Oxford University Press, 1989)

MT   Masoretic Text

NJBC   *New Jerome Biblical Commentary* (ed. R. Brown et al.; Englewood Cliffs, N.J.: Prentice-Hall, 1990)

15

ABBREVIATIONS

NRSV   New Revised Standard Version
SBLDS   Society of Biblical Literature Dissertation Series
SBLMS   Society of Biblical Literature Monograph Series
TUAT *Texte aus der Umwelt des Alten Testaments.* (Gütersloh: Mohn, 1990). Band III. Lieferung 1. Weisheitstexte I
ZAW   *Zeitschrift für die alttestamentliche Wissenschaft*

CHAPTER 1

OUR QUEST AND THE
BIBLE'S WISDOM

The term "wisdom literature" refers to the books of Proverbs, Job, Qoheleth, and sometimes the Song of Songs. Sirach and the Wisdom of Solomon are among the Apocrypha, the Protestant term for honored but noncanonical books. They are accepted as canonical by Roman Catholics and the Orthodox. Some authors want to include some psalms, such as 1, 32, 34, 37, 49, 112, and 128, under the same umbrella because "wisdom themes" appear in them. The wisdom books are traditionally grouped together because of their association with Solomon (Prov 1:1; 10:1; 25:1; Qoh 1:1; Cant 1:1) and because of their common themes and style. It is in fact useful to read them together, for one can more clearly see their common themes and subtle differences.

INITIAL REACTIONS TO BIBLICAL WISDOM

A first-time serious reading of the wisdom books brings many reactions. You will probably experience a mix of interest, confusion, boredom, and aversion. Your interest will be piqued by the occasional familiar or witty proverb, "One's folly subverts one's way, but one's anger rages against the Lord." Some of Job's eloquent tirades and his touching surrender may have the same effect.

> I have heard of you by the hearing of the ears,
>   but now my eye sees you.
> Therefore, I retract
>   and give up my dust and ashes. (42:5-6 my translation)

Qoheleth's meditation on "times" in a person's life is equally memorable.

> For everything there is a season, and a time for every matter under heaven:
> a time to be born, and a time to die;
> a time to plant, and a time to pluck up what is planted;
> a time to kill, and a time to heal;
> a time to break down, and a time to build up;
> a time to weep, and a time to laugh. (3:1-4a)

Not everything is so immediately gripping. The reader will likely be confused by Wisdom's speeches in Proverbs (why are they so vague?), the precise point of Yahweh's thunderous speeches to Job (Job 38–41), and the philosophical critique of pagan worship in Wisdom of Solomon 13–15. Many readers are put off by the seeming banality of many of Proverbs' sayings, the portrait of a testing God in Job, and the misogyny of Ben Sira.

Not only the content but the style of much of wisdom literature attracts and repels. The opening and closing lines of Qoheleth, "Vanity of vanities! All is vanity" seem timeless and right; God's speeches in Job are grand even in translation; the description of wisdom in Wisdom of Solomon 7:22b–8:1 is magnificent. On the other hand, the endless sayings in Proverbs and the seemingly heavy moral essays in Sirach can be very unappealing.

Though the wisdom literature can seem strange to us, it is important to realize that its concerns are modern; in fact they are our concerns. The best route to that realization is reading each book on its own terms. The rest of this chapter will be taken up with the first task—recognizing that the concerns of wisdom literature are modern, in fact our own. The second task—learning to see each book on its own terms—will be the task of subsequent chapters.

18

MODERN WISDOM LITERATURE

Is there such a thing as modern wisdom literature? The answer is yes, and a broad spectrum of its topics corresponds to biblical concerns. Hundreds of books and magazine articles deal with the topics of succeeding in business, handling relationships (friendships, colleagues at work), managing a family and household, learning to bear with equanimity life's pains and uncertainties, becoming a better person, making wise decisions, and reflections on such questions as God's presence in suffering, determinism and free will. Characteristic of the books and articles is their highly personal perspective. Missing from them are politics, economics, and history as well as national and international affairs, for these are not (for the most part) subject to *personal* decision and reflection. Wisdom literature is personal and familial.

The literature of the modern quest for wisdom has a variety of genres. One of the most common is biography and autobiography, which tell how one man or woman has been successful in surmounting life's difficulties or attaining a new level of insight. Another genre is advice, whether it be advice for succeeding in business, managing the home, or simply being a better person. Yet another genre is the collection or anthology, whether it be proverbs, quotations, or anecdotes.

These genres are only some of those found in today's "wisdom literature." Corresponding to each is an ancient genre, a reminder of how close the ancient and modern quests can be. For example, autobiography has similarities to Qoheleth, who the reader is supposed to assume is the great king Solomon reflecting on his life. Ben Sira in 51:13-22 ends his teaching with an autobiographical poem, a reminder that the book is not just any collection but one that has been tested by Ben Sira himself. He is, he tells us, "a canal from a river [wisdom]"; and "I have not labored for myself alone, / but for all who seek wisdom" (24:30, 34).

Other genres have ancient precedents. Our modern moral tales, lists of do's and don'ts, and inventories of the habits of successful people can all be found in various guises in the Bible and beyond. And that most pervasive wisdom genre, the proverb or aphorism, is found in virtually all cultures in every age. Even in third-millennium Sumer twenty-four books of proverbs are attested.

A river of wisdom has flowed from the earliest records of the human race to the present. People have always sought to understand, to go beyond their first and often mistaken impressions to a more profound level of truth. They have sought to learn how to respond to reality, to act in a wise way, to do what brings them and others happiness and success. The Bible is the inspired attempt to become wise at the deepest level.

BIBLICAL WISDOM LITERATURE

The book of Proverbs is an anthology of older collections of instructions and aphorisms and a number of short additions and poems. The instructions of chapters 1–9 inculcate trust in one's teachers and parents and recommend the energetic search for wisdom itself. In Proverbs, the search for and orientation toward wisdom is more important than learning specific things or doing a wise thing. From chapter 10 forward, the book consists largely of two-line aphorisms—exhortations, observations, paradoxes—designed, it seems, to aid the quest for wisdom. That search brings prosperity and happiness, because it puts one in touch with God and reveals the real structure of the world.

Job is the story of a legendary righteous man whose life suddenly goes awry when God (unbeknownst to Job) makes him a pawn in a wager with a mysterious heavenly figure. Job is systematically stripped of possessions and of family, after which we (and God) watch this paragon of virtue reacting to the counsel that his friends propose to him. He angrily refutes their wisdom and demands to meet God. God's thunderous response stops Job in his tracks, but, to everybody's surprise, God declares Job righteous, restoring his lost goods and providing him a new family.

Job in one sense is a biography—how one man faced disintegration with dignity and came back from the brink. The book resembles today's stories of struggle and triumph that inspire us, yet it is obviously far more than a biography. More than anything it is an inquiry into the nature of God, human beings, and the created world.

Qoheleth contains the reflections of a great king in his maturity, reflecting on what he has learned about life. His sense of the uncertainties of life (especially in commerce) and the inevitability of death have taught him flexibility toward tradition and the advisability of enjoying the present moment. He is a skeptic ("vanity" is a favorite word) but not a nihilist. For him, traditional wisdom is insufficient unless its application to the ever-shifting and unknowable present can be identified.

The book of Sirach is a great collection of essays in poetic form. Ben Sira in the early second century is self-consciously a sage and heir to what had become in his lifetime a considerable body of wisdom teaching. His teaching ranges from proper household management in the face of newfangled ideas to discussing controversial issues such as the ultimate origin of evil (from God or human beings?) and how wisdom has appeared in the history of Israel. He has a mastery of the entire tradition and attempts to synthesize it in a persuasive manner.

Ben Sira, avoiding the dissenting voices of Job and Qoheleth, weaves the old aphorisms into moral essays, leaving behind the old elliptical and paradoxical style to create a more logical and discursive literature. His book is a library in which one can wander and discover the old tradition in new dress.

The book of Wisdom was not written on Palestinian soil and uses Greek rather than Hebrew modes of expression. The Jewish community in Egypt was in trouble, pressed by its Egyptian neighbors. The book attempts to give the community the confidence it had lost. Our Jewish wisdom, says the author, is a manifestation of the hidden power that rules the world. Wisdom picks agents or witnesses in every age (Solomon being the great exemplar), enters such people, and enables them to understand that the real, abiding world is hidden, yet will be triumphant. This world appears especially when the innocent righteous are killed and exalted. The old story of Israel in Egypt offers a way of understanding how the holy community is to live now.

These are the wisdom books, collected or written by human beings like ourselves. In one sense, the authors are highly conservative, for they revere the tradition, which they have studied carefully. In another sense, however, they are highly innovative and even on occasion rebellious, for they also revere their own experience and honestly record their impressions. The books look alike in many respects, but each is unique. And the genius of each becomes clearer the more each book is studied.

RECOMMENDED READING

General Introductions

Bergant, Dianne. *Israel's Wisdom Literature.* Minneapolis: Fortress, 1997. A study of all the wisdom books using "the integrity of creation" as the basic perspective.

Clifford, Richard J. "Introduction to Wisdom Literature," in *The New Interpreter's Bible,* vol. 5. Nashville: Abingdon Press, 1997, pp. 1-16.

Crenshaw, James L. *Old Testament Wisdom: An Introduction.* Atlanta: John Knox, 1981. A standard introduction.

Murphy, Roland E. *The Tree of Life: An Exploration of Biblical Wisdom Literature.* 2nd ed. Grand Rapids, Mich.: Eerdmans, 1996. Excellent introduction to wisdom literature and up-to-date survey of the chief scholarly issues, and bibliography.

————. "Wisdom in the OT," in the *Anchor Bible Dictionary,* vol. 6. New York: Doubleday, 1992. Pp. 920-31. A balanced presentation. The *Anchor Bible Dictionary* is a fine resource, with articles on all the biblical wisdom books and principal topics.

Perdue, Leo G. *Wisdom and Creation: The Theology of Wisdom Literature.* Nashville: Abingdon Press, 1994. A fine survey of recent work on theology and an integration of theological and literary approaches.

von Rad, Gerhard. *Wisdom in Israel.* Nashville/New York: Abingdon Press, 1972. A groundbreaking work, full of theological insights and extremely influential on theological discussion of wisdom literature.

Studies

Barré, Michael L. " 'Fear of God' and the World View of Wisdom," *BTB* 11 (1981): 41-43. Effectively argues that ancient wisdom was always religious, against some recent scholarship.

Crenshaw, James L., ed. *Studies in Ancient Israelite Wisdom.* New York: KTAV, 1976. Influential scholarly essays.

————. *Theodicy in the Old Testament.* Philadelphia: Fortress, 1983. Essays, some not previously in English, on the problem of God's wisdom and justice in the world.

Murphy, Roland E. *The Forms of Old Testament Literature.* Forms of Old Testament Literature 13. Grand Rapids: Eerdmans, 1981. Form-critical analysis of all the wisdom books.

CHAPTER 2

WISDOM LITERATURE IN THE ANCIENT NEAR EAST

Israel, on the evidence of the Bible itself, was a small nation in the Levant of the late-second and first millennia B.C.E. It was surrounded by small nations and peoples, some of them closely related in culture and language. To the north during the tenth to the eighth centuries were Aramaean city states. And there were the great empires that loomed over Israel: Egypt during almost its entire history, Neo-Assyria (eighth and seventh centuries), Neo-Babylon (late-seventh and early sixth centuries), Persia (539–333 B.C.E.), the Seleucid and Ptolemaic empires (333–164 B.C.E.). These nations had their own literatures and customs. They also had a relationship to Israel through trade, diplomacy, or military occupation. It is not surprising, therefore, that biblical writings show the influence of other literatures.

The Bible is not a collection of private writings but an anthology of literary works that served a role in the political and liturgical life of the Israelite people. It was as much marked by the peculiar history and culture of the people as it was by the individual genius of its authors. Biblical literature was therefore inevitably interna-

23

tional. Its genres appear elsewhere in the ancient East. In the last two centuries of the modern era much of the literature of Israel's neighbors has been recovered in excavations and by chance finds. Hundreds of thousands of clay tablets have been dug up in Mesopotamia and Syria; inscribed sherds and monuments have been excavated in Palestine; and papyri and inscribed boards have been recovered in Egypt. Texts long known have been restudied in the light of new knowledge. The texts show beyond a doubt that authors in Israel chose to write in types or genres that were common elsewhere. Chronicles, hymns, laments, stories about ancient heroes, laws, liturgical regulations, prophecies, love songs, proverbs, instructions, theological disputes, skeptical literature—all these genres show up in the Bible. The biblical law codes are a particularly good instance of borrowing and interchange, for example, Exodus 21:1-23; Leviticus 17–26; Deuteronomy 12–26. At one time, Israel's law codes were thought to be unique, but we now have other important collections of cuneiform law for comparison: the Sumerian laws of Ur Nammu and Lipit Ishtar, the Old Babylonian laws of Eshnunna and Hammurabi, the Middle Assyrian laws from Asshur, the Hittite law code, and a small collection of Late Babylonian laws. They represent a common law tradition, which, despite local variations, was essentially shared throughout the region of Mesopotamia, Syria, and Palestine. The very act of making collections of laws was part of the common tradition. A specific example of the communality is the law about the goring ox in Exodus 21:28-36: the same problem is also dealt with in the laws of Eshnunna 53-55 and Hammurabi 250-52. Comparing all three instances leads to the conclusion that the Bible does not have a superior evaluation of human life as once was thought, for respect for life was part of the ancient legal tradition.[1] Another example is the creation-flood story in Genesis 2–11, which draws on the Akkadian epics *Atrahasis* and *Gilgamesh*.[2] Even the prophets, who have always been reckoned as uniquely Israelite, have forebears.

Comparing literatures is a difficult task. Without discipline or good method, parallels will be found everywhere. In comparing ancient literature with the Bible two principles must be kept in mind. The first is that the purpose of comparison is not to prove the Bible superior to other literature or prove it is "true," but rather to help us understand the biblical passage. The law of the goring ox is a good example. The laws of Eshnunna or Hammurabi enable us to see that the case was enshrined in ancient common law and was not peculiar to Israelite law. One can recognize the beauty and truth in other literatures without lowering one's estimate of the grandeur of the Bible.

The second principle in comparing ancient literature and the Bible is that it is more productive to compare genres and wholes than individual items and odd details. Genre is important in the literature of any age, for knowing beforehand what we are reading gives us a general sense of location, enabling us to see the new and the traditional in a passage. In other words, writers compose and readers read within conventions; otherwise literature could not be understood. Understanding the genre of a particular piece, such as a lyric poem, a liturgical lament, a creation-flood story, enables one to understand the conventions of *this* lyric poem, lament, and creation-flood story.[3] Biblical wisdom literature contains several genres that occur again and again: instructions of a father or parents to a son, proverbs, riddles, witty sayings. Some genres, such as the disputation on divine justice, are associated with only one book, in this case Job.

Thus, to understand biblical literature, it is helpful to examine the non-Israelite wisdom literature. First, comparable literature in Mesopotamia, Egypt, and Canaan is surveyed. Next, a look will be taken at representative samples in translation to show the quality of the works and the process into which they invite the reader.

MESOPOTAMIA

Before examining the extant wisdom literature, we should note an important assumption about wisdom made by the ancient authors—its hierarchical nature. Since this assumption runs counter to our modern view of wisdom in daily life, a word of explanation is necessary. This consideration is especially helpful for understanding the instructions. Ancient writers assumed that wisdom belonged to the gods. All the gods can occasionally be called "wise," but one in particular, Ea (Enki in the Sumerian language) is so wise as to be the counselor of the gods. He is the one who proposed the creation of the human race to serve the gods and he is concerned with their survival. But other heavenly and even earthly beings shared in divine wisdom. In Mesopotamian mythology the seven sages *(apkallu)*, who mediated knowledge and culture to the human race before the flood, were succeeded in the post-flood era by four sages, according to some ritual texts. The post-flood sages are called *ummānu*, "scholars," in some texts, and that title will surface again when we discuss Proverbs 8. The four sages are associated in one text with a human king and the last is expressly called a human being. This myth explains how it is that writings—liturgy, science, magic, and belles lettres—are the work of the wise. At the head of gods and heavenly beings ultimately stands the god Enki or Ea; from him the line of wisdom descends through the *apkallu* and *ummānu* down to human scholars; the human contribution grows progressively greater as the line descends. At the end of the chain of wisdom is the Babylonian school, which is run by the learned sages.⁴ Wisdom belongs to the gods and there must be a process so that it can be given to others. In the chain of transmission in Mesopotamia, scribes are in a line going back to Ea. Wisdom comes to human beings mediated by authorities in the community such as kings, teachers, and parents. To say that God or the gods give wisdom does not mean that it is given unmediated. The important thing is that wisdom is given from on high; how it was mediated was less important. The same process, allowing for local differences, would be true of Canaan.

W. G. Lambert observes at the beginning of his magisterial *Babylonian Wisdom Literature*, "Though [wisdom literature] is thus foreign to ancient Mesopotamia, it has been used for a group of texts which correspond in subject matter with the Hebrew Wisdom books, and may be retained as a short description."⁵ Students of ancient Mesopotamia sometimes broaden the category "wisdom literature" beyond the biblical works. For the volume on wisdom literature in the Sumerian language, in the series "Texts from the Environment of the Old Testament," Willem H. Ph. Römer includes genres not found in the Bible: fables and riddles, "school satires" such as a father's berating of his son's performance in school, and disputations in a school setting. A considerable amount of Sumerian wisdom literature did not interest Akkadian scribes of a later era. At any rate they did not copy the entire repertory but only certain types. Lambert notes "the curious phenomenon that [proverbs] do not seem to have become part of stock literature."⁶ Precepts and admonitions fared better. The Instructions of Shuruppak was copied and the "Counsels of Wisdom" (about 160 moral exhortations) was a popular text.

Two Mesopotamian genres, the instruction and the proverb, are of particular interest. Mesopotamian examples of both genres must have been known to Israelite scribes. The oldest and most widely known instruction is the Instruction of Shuruppak, in which Shuruppak gives his son Ziusudra rules of behavior and wise counsel.[7] Ziusudra was the Sumerian equivalent of biblical Noah. The son is the customary recipient of ancient instructions.

[1]In that [day], in that far off day,
in that [ni]ght, in that far dista[nt] night,
in that [year], in that far distant year—
at that time there lived one who possessed wisdom, who (with) artful
words, who knew the (right) word, in the land of Sumer,
[5]Shuruppak lived, who possessed wisdom, who (with) artful words,
who knew the (right) word, in the land of Sumer.
Shuruppak counseled his son,
Shuruppak, the son of Uburtutu,
[10]counseled Ziusudra, his son:
"My son, I will counsel (you), may my counsel be accepted,
Ziusudra, a word will I s[ay] to you, may it be heeded!
Do not neglect my counsel,
the word that I have spoken, do not change,
the counsel of a father is precious, may your neck bow before it."

The counsels that follow are from one to three lines in length. The Old Babylonian version of the Instructions of Shuruppak has 281 lines and is divided into three sections (lines 1-76, 77-146, 147-281). Each section begins elaborately with language similar to that in the main introduction; each concludes with a formula, "[Thus] Shuruppak advised his son," or the like. Different recensions of the work (two in the third millennium and an Old Babylonian edition) show variety. The counsels are varied; some are simply farming advice: [17]"Do not put a well in the midst of a field; the water will do damage to you"; others are witty observations: [95-97]"The palace is like a mighty river, its insides are like butting oxen; its income is never enough, its expenses never end"; others are genuinely proverbial: [31]"My son, do not commit murder; do not split yourself with an axe!" The elaborate introduction, repeated twice in the course of the counsels, serves to place the varied sayings under the imposing mantle of the primordial hero Shuruppak and his equally legendary son Ziusudra, the wise hero of the flood. The language of the introduction ("in that day, in that far-off day") is conventional for describing primordial time; it introduces Sumerian cosmogonies. In the worldview of Mesopotamia, things were better in the ancient pre-flood past than in the present; there was greater wisdom and vitality then than there is now. Wisdom was understood hierarchically; the gods were preeminently wise and communicated their wisdom to heroes and kings who then communicated it to others.

Unfortunately, many of Shuruppak's instructions are obscure. The Sumerian language is imperfectly known, the tablets are often fragmentary, and many of the allusions escape us. The following sayings are typical and worth pondering, both in their own right and as points of comparison with the Bible. It is worth asking whether they offer advice applicable only to one situation or can be read metaphorically (saying one thing in terms of another). Do you detect wit and humor? Can you distinguish admonitions, exhortations, observations, and maxims (proverbs)?

[18]Do not build a house in the square; the crowd is (there).

[19]Do not make a guarantee (for someone); the person will have a hold on you.

[22-23]Do not go to a place of strife; / the strife will make you a witness.

[30]The thief is a lion; after he is caught he is a slave!

[51]You should not curse with violence: it comes back to the hand!

[63]Do not rape a man's daughter; she will announce it to the courtyard.

[64-65]Do not drive away a strong man; do not destroy a city wall; / do not drive away a guruš-worker, do not turn him away from the city!

[66-67]A slanderer spins his eyes as if with a spindle; / do not stand before his eyes: he changes the judgment of his heart again and again.

[98-101]With regard to another man's bread, "I will give it to you" is near,[8] / (but) to give it is far heaven's span. / (Even if you say) "I will urge upon the man (the promise) 'I will give it to you,'" / he will not give it to you: the bread has already been consumed.

[152-54]Regarding harvesttime, the very precious days, / collect like a slave girl, eat like a lady, / my son,[9] eat like a slave girl, eat like a lady—thus shall it be indeed.

[171-72]Fate is like a wet riverbank; / it makes a person's feet slip.

[173-75]The older brother is actually (like) a father, the older sister is actually (like) a mother! / may you heed your older brother, / may you bend your neck to your older sister for the sake of your mother.

Most of the sentences are counsels to perform or not perform a specific act for a stated reason (18, 19, 22-23, 51, 63, 64-65, 132-34, 173-75). Several can be classed as observations (66-67, 98-101, 171-72). The advice is not as specific and detailed as that of Egyptian instructions. Some of it is blunt, "farmer's almanac" talk (18, 19) but most is indirect, metaphorical. Nearly all the counsels have a command and a reason, for example, [63]"Do not rape a man's daughter; she will announce it to the courtyard." As is very clear from the example, the rationale need not be moral but can be pure self-interest, the trouble that follows a crime.

The Counsels of Wisdom is a collection of about 160 moral exhortations, dated by Lambert to the Kassite period (ca. 1500–1200 B.C.E.).[10] It is addressed to "my son." "Son" is the typical recipient of instructions in the ancient Near East though the expression "my son" seems to be used regularly only in the Bible and Mesopotamian wisdom literature. There is a series of topics (some in different meters): avoidance of bad companions, improper speech, avoiding strife and placating enemies (31-55?), being kind to the needy, the danger of favoring a slave girl, the danger of marrying a prostitute, the trustworthiness required of a representative, the importance of courteous speech, the duties and benefits of religion.

> [21]Don't stop to talk with a frivolous person,
>   Nor go consult with a [ ] who has nothing to do.
>   With good intentions you will do their thinking for them,
>   You will diminish your own accomplishment, abandon your own
>   course.
>   You will play false to your own, wiser, thinking.

> [26]Hold your tongue, watch what you say.
>   A man's pride: the great value on your lips.
>   Insolence and insult should be abhorrent to you.
>   Speak nothing slanderous, no untrue report.
>   The frivolous person is of no account.

The motive given in line 21 and line 26 for avoiding frivolous companions is that they harm one's standing in the community by lessening the value of what one says. Lambert translates, "Therein is a man's wealth—let your lips be very precious." The penalty one pays is stated in the last line, "The talebearer [Lambert's translation] is of no account." Proverbs also counsels people to avoid evil companions on similar grounds (22:24-25; 23:17; 24:1).

Lines 31-55 warn against getting embroiled in strife and conclude with advice on how to deal with an enemy.

> [42]Do no evil to the man who disputes with you,
>   Requite with good the one who does evil to you.

Be fair to your enemy,
Let your mood be cheerful to your opponent.
Be it your ill-wisher, tre[at him generous]ly.
Make up your mind to no evil,
Suc[h is not] acceptable [to the] gods,
Evil [   ] is abhorrent to [   ] Marduk.

The context is the danger of disputes, which can pull one into trouble. Means of avoidance include placating enemies and forswearing revenge. Planning evil against another is not acceptable to the god Marduk. The "Counsels," like Proverbs, mention gods by their name. Similar counsel against exacting vengeance is expressed in Proverbs 24:17-18 and especially 25:21-22, "If your enemies are hungry, give them bread to eat; / and if they are thirsty, give them water to drink; / for you will heap coals of fire on their heads, / and the LORD will reward you." In the Babylonian *Counsels,* planning evil against another, even one who has inflicted some wrong on the person planning the vengeance, can offend the gods. The Proverbs text also forbids exacting vengeance and gives the rationale—exacting vengeance is a divine not a human task.

The last sample concerns a suitable marriage partner, which is also a concern of Proverbs.

[72]Don't marry a prostitute, whose husbands are legion,
Nor a temple harlot, who is dedicated to a goddess,
Nor a courtesan, whose intimates are numerous.
She will not sustain you in your time of trouble,
She will snigger at you when you are embroiled in controversy.
She has neither respect nor obedience in her nature.
Even if she has the run of your house, get rid of her,
She has ears attuned for another's footfall.

The implicit criterion for a marriage partner in these counsels is loyalty; none of the candidates for marriage listed has the capacity for unlimited loyalty to one husband. "Respect" and "obedience" are aspects of the affectionate fidelity sought in a spouse. Proverbs and Egyptian instructions both warn against dalliance with a "foreign" or forbidden woman, for she will destroy the marriage. Unlike the *Counsels,* however, Proverbs does not warn against marrying into any specific *class.*

Another common Mesopotamian genre was the proverb collection; more than twenty-four collections of Sumerian proverbs are attested. The collections include other material such as fables, witty expressions, raillery, and jokes. The purpose of the *collections* (not the individual sayings) may have been to teach the Sumerian language and its rhetoric and, in the process, to teach practical wisdom to the young students who studied and copied them. Most of the sayings are from the Old Babylonian period (ca. 1800–1600 B.C.E.). The Sumerian proverbs are exceedingly difficult for modern readers, because Sumerian is incompletely known and because the cultural context escapes us.

Reprinted here are some Sumerian proverbs from collections 7 and 1. The proverbs introduce readers to their concerns and their rhetoric.[11] My interpretation, in some cases quite tentative, is given following the texts.

7.14A hairdresser is dressed in an unwashed garment.

7.15I drink thin beer, I will sit in the place of honor.

7.33He quickly went and slaughtered his pig, he quickly went and used up his wood.

7.49I run around, I am not tired, I run around, I do not sleep.

7.77"Alas," he said. The boat sank. To that he said, "A bucket!" The rudder broke off. The man said, "Alas, O God." Then the boat came near its destination.

7.98Good is the beer, bad is the expedition.

1.105Who continually drinks beer, will continually drink water.

1.160To marry a wife is (a thing) of a man, (but) to have children is (a thing) of God.

The term "proverbs" is obviously too narrow for these sayings. The items range from a vignette with a moral to an enigmatic saying; several display sardonic humor; others require the reader to interpret them.

Here are my interpretations, which readers may want to compare with their own. Sayings 7.14 and 7.15 are comic contrasts, a hairdresser who does not pay attention to his own appearance, and a poor person drinking the drink of the poor yet harboring grandiose ambitions; 7.33 illustrates the folly of preferring luxuries to essentials, or squandering precious resources; 7.49 may be a riddle: who is it that does such a thing? 7.77 is a little story showing that reliance on the gods is more effective than reliance on self; 7.98 is a humorous statement that people prefer comfort to exertion ("expedition" is either military or commercial); 1:160 is an aphorism on human limit and on divine power.

31

The instructions and aphorisms examined here give some sense of didactic and aphoristic literature in Mesopotamia. Other compositions in the Akkadian language are relevant to biblical wisdom literature, but they are peculiar to one biblical book and will be examined in the chapter dealing with that work. They include *I will praise the Lord of Wisdom* (= *Ludlul bēl nēmeqi*), *A Man and His God*, *Prayer of a Sufferer* (from Ugarit), *The Babylonian Theodicy*, and *A Pessimistic Dialog.*

MESOPOTAMIAN SOCIAL LOCATION

In addition to providing "wisdom" genres comparable to those in the Bible, Mesopotamian texts inform us about the literary world in which the texts were written.[12] Such knowledge is all the more valuable in that the Bible supplies little information about authors and social location. We do not know, for example, who wrote the biblical wisdom books, what institution sponsored their copying and distribution, and who read them. Were there wisdom schools? Were they written by village elders, or by court scribes? Mesopotamian texts give an answer to these questions: its literature is found entirely within the world of the scribes. It is significant that there is only one Akkadian term for scribe, *ṭupšarru*, despite all their specializations. They wrote the literature and saw to its transmission. Literature was by definition what *they* copied and stocked in libraries. Their copying of only certain texts accounts for multiple copies of the limited number of works in the stream of tradition. Scribes had three roles—bureaucrat, poet, and scholar. As bureaucrats they recorded the intake and outflow of palace goods; as poets they composed literary works such as hymns, epics, annals, inscriptions, and the like; as scholars they recorded and arranged omens and practiced divination. The most important institution for the production of literature was the royal court, for the temple had yielded its economic and political importance to the palace. The king sponsored scribes and paid for their literary production, accepting it as part of his responsibility to maintain political and economic order and stability.

Unlike the situation in other societies, Mesopotamian scribes were not by virtue of their office connected with sanctuaries or other religious institutions, nor did they operate within a body of normative or "classical" texts. They functioned within the palace organization or, with the increased economic prosperity of the first millennium B.C.E., independently, selling their "scholarly" services (omens and divination) to wealthy individuals.

EGYPT

Literature comparable to the biblical wisdom books was composed as early as the mid-third millennium, though there is no single term like "wisdom literature" to describe it. Egyptologists sometimes group three important genres under the rubric "wisdom": instructions, laments or complaints, and political propaganda. Of the three, instructions and complaints are relevant to the Bible.

The instructions provide much information on their own history and social context.[13] The instruction was a live genre during the entire history of ancient Egypt; seventeen examples from different periods are extant. The oldest is the *Instruction of Prince Hardjedef*, composed ca. 2450–2300 B.C.E. (*AEL*, vol. 1, pp. 58-59), and the latest is *Papyrus Insinger* of the first century C.E., which is written in Demotic, the vernacular language (*AEL*, vol. 3, pp. 184-217). One instruction, the *Instruction of Amenemope* of ca. 1100 B.C.E. (*ANET*, pp. 421-25; *AEL*, vol. 2, pp. 146-63), is generally acknowledged to have directly influenced Proverbs 22:17–24:22.

Egyptian instructions aimed to enable a young person to lead a happy and prosperous life, free of undue difficulties and costly mistakes. They proffer concrete and pragmatic suggestions rather than hold up abstract ideals to which one should measure up. A good example of their approach is: don't lie to a judge, for telling the truth will render the judge benevolent the next time around; in the long run lies do not work in any case. The pragmatism and self-interest of such counsels should not be taken, however, as proof that Egyptian instructions were secular. On the contrary, they were always thoroughly religious. Like other ancient peoples, Egyptians believed that the gods implanted order, which they called *maat*, in the world.[14] *Maat* can be translated with different English words—truth, order, justice. It is found in nature (the seasons, fruitfulness) no less than in the human world (civic and social order, laws, right relationships within families and professions, among neighbors, and in relation to the king). In Egyptian mythology, *Maat* is the daughter of Re, the god of the sun and of justice;

she is portrayed crouching with a feather on her knees or head. *Maat* was not revealed but "read off" the course of the world and communicated through the maxims and exhortations of instructions. To help readers fulfill the demands of *maat* in every walk of life was the aim of the instructions. Some scholars see *maat* as the model for personified Wisdom in Proverbs. The analogy is possible, but Wisdom in Proverbs displays a vigor and a personality in pursuit of her lovers that goes far beyond the abstract Egyptian goddess. Finally, the aim of the instructions is to guide the individual rather than to reform society; readers accepted the world as it was and sought to live according to its rhythms. The instructions advocate not changing the world but helping individuals adapt themselves to it.

Some aspects of the instructions are explained by their context in Egyptian society. The career of the young person was played out, at least initially, within the *famulus* (private secretary) system; one entered the household of high officials (mostly of royal blood) who trained their successors in their household. The system was not peculiar to Egypt; Joseph in the book of Genesis and Ahiqar were "private secretaries" or courtiers. The young person served the great personage, establishing a solid relationship, like Joseph with Potiphar (Gen 39:2) and Pharaoh (Gen 41:40). In the course of history, formal classes came to be conducted at the royal court. In the world of apprenticeship, fidelity to one's master was paramount. The *famulus* system explains the emphasis on delivering messages accurately, avoiding (domestic) quarrels, and guarding against entanglements with women of the household.

In portraying human beings the instructions use "heart" as the seat of feeling and especially of intelligence. A "hard-hearted" person lacks good sense not compassion. The portrayal of the human scene was dramatic: human beings are characterized by a fundamental polarity—the wise person and the fool, the heated and the silent person. Fools do not follow the advice of their "father" or elder and thus do not act according to *maat*. The cleverness of the wise is the result of education, nature, and their own shrewd assessment of people and situations. "Hearing" (in the sense of heeding) is an important verb in the exhortations. Egyptian society was open, allowing poor and ambitious young people to rise to positions of power. People from the provinces or from poor households did not know the ropes and needed guidebooks in order to attain success.

Instructions were composed throughout the three millennia of Egyptian history and reflect changes in society. The genre arose with the beginning of the Egyptian state in the third millennium, when the need to administer vast territories required the king's servants to leave behind their village routine, to travel, and to respond to situations beyond their experience. Instructions of the Old Kingdom (2650–2135 B.C.E.) revolved around the king, but with the decline of kingship and the social disorder of the First Intermediate Period (2135–2040 B.C.E.) the instructions turned away from royal affairs to private concerns. With the restoration of stable monarchy in the Middle Kingdom (2040–1650 B.C.E.), they once again stress loyalty to the king. New Kingdom authors came from all levels of society, for daily business was now conducted by a broad range of people. With the *Instruction of Any* in the Eighteenth Dynasty (ca. 1550–1305 B.C.E.), concern for the individual and the acquiring of inner peace reappears and dominates the genre down to Hellenistic and Roman times. A good indication of societal change is the way success was interpreted. In the Old Kingdom, when courtiers were the intended readers, success meant getting ahead at court. When the readership became less tied to a particular class, exhortations became more general and more personal— how to avoid suffering, conflicts, and disappointments in life.

Contrary to the anonymity of Egyptian art, the instructions name their authors, presenting them as real people—kings or prominent scribes. The authority of instructions, after all, rested on the repute of their writers no less than on their antiquity. Reverence for authority and for antiquity did not, however, prevent subsequent editors from recasting and rearranging the ancient wisdom as they transmitted it.

We turn now to samples of Egyptian instructions, beginning with an introduction to a section in the *Instruction of Amenemope* (ca. 1100 B.C.E.), using Lichtheim's translations.

Give your ears, hear the sayings,
Give your heart to understand them;
It profits to put them in your heart;
Woe to him who neglects them!
Let them rest in the casket of your belly;
May they be bolted in your heart.
When there rises a whirlwind of words,
They'll be a mooring post for your tongue.

If you make your life with these in your heart,
You will find it a success;
You will find my words a storehouse for life;
Your being will prosper upon earth. (III.9–IV.2)[15]

The passage bears some resemblance to the wisdom lectures in Proverbs 1–9, which typically urge the youth to hear and memorize the teacher's words as the first step in acquiring wisdom. In the course of time these words turn into wisdom, maxims for action, as they are acted upon.

An example of the warm humanity, fear of "heated" quarreling, and shrewd self-interest is an excerpt from section 4 of the *Instruction of Ptahhotep* (Sixth Dynasty, ca. 2300–2150).

If you meet a disputant in action,
A poor man, not your equal,
Do not attack him because he is weak,
Let him alone, he will confute himself.
Do not answer him to relieve your heart,
Do not vent yourself against your opponent,
Wretched is he who injures a poor man,
One will wish to do what you desire,
You will beat him through the magistrates' reproof.[16]

From the *Instruction of Amenemope* comes a warning against avarice, which has influenced Proverbs 23:4–5.

Do not set your heart on wealth,
There is no ignoring Fate and Destiny;
Do not let your heart go straying,
Every man comes to his hour.
Do not strain to seek increase,
What you have, let it suffice you.
If riches come to you by theft,
They will not stay the night with you.
Comes day they are not in your house,
Their place is seen but they're not there;
Earth opened its mouth, leveled them, swallowed them,
and made them sink into *dat*.
They made a hole as big as their size,
And sank into the netherworld;
They made themselves wings like geese,
And flew away to the sky.[17]

36

The *Instruction of Amenemope* warns against setting one's heart on wealth, for destiny and fate, which can rip away all gain, are beyond our control; stolen property disappears into primordial nothingness *(dat)*, making wings for itself to fly off to the sky. Proverbs 23:4-5 develops the imagery of fleeting birds and wealth by imagining avaricious intent itself as a flight of the eyes: "Do not wear yourself out to get rich; / be wise enough to desist. / When your eyes light upon it, it is gone; / for suddenly it takes wings to itself, flying like an eagle toward heaven." These examples must suffice as illustrations of the imagination and intelligence that Proverbs uses as it makes use of Egyptian material.

EGYPTIAN SOCIAL LOCATION

What was the social location of Egyptian "wisdom literature"? Composing, studying, teaching, and copying texts took place in a kind of academy known as the House of Life, which was usually located near temples and had a role in worship. Instructions were copied out by schoolchildren to learn the Egyptian script; their sometimes faulty copies are often the chief manuscript source for instructions. Instructions were never meant to be school texts, however. The addressee in instructions was a "son," which is broader than "son" in English: it expressed any close relationship with a younger person—one's child, student, or successor. The texts contain a high degree of emotion, for the prestige of the "father" depended on the success of the "son." The instructions were class-specific up to the first millennium, at which time formulations became more general.

At the very end of the third millennium another type of writing appeared, which was less a genre than a general style of pessimistic and cynical attacks on traditional ways of thinking. *The Admonitions of Ipuwer (ANET,* 441-44; *AEL,* vol. 1, pp. 159-63), after a grim recital of the troubles of the land (a common topos), blames the creator-god using the form of dialogue. *The Tale of the Eloquent Peasant (ANET,* 407-10; *AEL,* vol. 1, pp. 169-84) is a confrontation in nine speeches between a peasant and a high official. Harper's songs *(ANET,* 467; *AEL,* vol. 1, pp. 194-97) urge readers to enjoy today for who knows about tomorrow. *The Satire on the Trades (ANET,* 432-34; *AEL,* vol. 1, pp. 184-92) criticizes nonscribal activities in order to glorify the profession of scribe. *The Dispute of a*

37

Person with his Ba (= vital force; *ANET,* 405-7; *AEL,* vol. 1, pp. 163-69) vividly describes the miseries of life. These works show that scribes in Egypt were as free as those in Mesopotamia to criticize the tradition. One should not regard skeptical works ipso facto as the products of alienated or marginalized groups. They could arise from within the center of the scribal guild. The questioning and satirical spirit of the biblical books of Job and Ecclesiastes has good analogues in Egypt.

CANAAN

Egypt and Mesopotamia are geographically distant from the Levant, Israel's homeland, and culturally different. Is there wisdom literature from Israel's own homeland and culture? The peoples of the Levant shared a common literary tradition, and a northern sample of it is provided by the late-second-millennium alphabetic cuneiform texts, which have been excavated from the city of Ugarit in present-day Syria. Unfortunately, few wisdom texts have been found at the site, and most of them are Babylonian: the *Counsels of Shube Awilum (BM,* 332-35), collections of sayings, and a hymn of trust to Marduk (similar to the Babylonian *I will praise the Lord of wisdom*). All are in the original Akkadian, showing that the Canaanite scribes of Ugarit read and appreciated Mesopotamian literature.

The most important nonbiblical "Canaanite" wisdom text is *Ahiqar,* which combines a narrative of the fall and subsequent restoration of the courtier Ahiqar with a collection of about a hundred aphorisms, riddles, fables, instructions, and graded numerical sayings. Ahiqar is attested elsewhere as an *ummānu,* a scholar and high official of King Esarhaddon of the Neo-Assyrian Empire (681–669 B.C.E.). His fall at the hands of his nephew Nadin and restoration to his former office may well have been based on historical fact, though the story is now fitted into the plot of the vindicated courtier, which is similar to the stories of Joseph, Esther, and Daniel. The narrative framework was written in Aramaic in the seventh century B.C.E.; it probably first circulated among Aramaic speakers in the Neo-Assyrian court. The sayings may be older, some possibly originating in the Aramaic kingdoms of Syria. It is noteworthy that the courtier Ahiqar, who has experienced many things and suffered much, is celebrated as the author of sayings, exhortations, and wisdom poems. Practical wisdom is connected to experience and shrewdness in bearing up under trials; Ahiqar has been through "discipline," a process of deprivation and humiliation from which he was rescued by God.

The framework story begins:[18] "[These are the wor]ds of one Ahiqar, a wise and skillful scribe, which he taught his son. N[ow *he did not have offspring of his own, but*] he said, 'I shall nevertheless have a son!' " The "son" of the childless Ahiqar is his nephew Nadin, who falsely accuses him of treason. Sentenced to death, Ahiqar goes into hiding, but in the course of time comes forward to provide the Egyptian king with his wisdom.

The following excerpts from the sayings are meant to give an idea of their range and style.

> [7.107]A king is like the Merciful;
>   even his voice is haughty.
>   Who is there who could withstand him,
>   but one with whom El is?[19]

The merciful king is Esarhaddon. One gets a sense of the awe felt toward the king in this and other passages: [7.100]"Quench not the word of a king; / let it be a balm [for] your [hea]rt." [7.101]"A king's word is gentle, but keener and more cutting than a double-edge dagger." This view of the king is standard in the ancient East. The Bible often subjects the king to a sharp prophetic critique but also witnesses to the traditional view as in Proverbs 24:21-22: "My child, fear the LORD and the king, / and do not disobey either of them; / for disaster comes from them suddenly, / and who knows the ruin that both can bring?"; 16:10: "Inspired decisions are on the lips of a king; / his mouth does not sin in judgment."

Graded numerical sayings are a feature of Canaanite style; they are found only in West Semitic literature. A Ugaritic instance is *KTU* 1.4.iii.17-21: "Two kinds of feasts Baal hates, three, the rider on the clouds—a feast of shame, a feast of meanness, and a feast where maids behave lewdly." Ahiqar 92: "There are two things which are good, / and a third which is pleasing to Shamash: / one who drinks wine and shares it, / one who masters wisdom *[and observes it]*; / and one who hears a word but tells it not." The same device is found in the Bible, in Proverbs 6:16-19: "There are six things that the LORD hates, / seven that are an abomination to him: / haughty eyes, a lying tongue, / and hands that shed innocent blood, / a heart that devises wicked plans, / feet that hurry to run to evil, / a lying witness who testifies falsely, / and one who sows discord in a family."

The final piece from Ahiqar is a personification of Wisdom (6.94–7.95), comparable to Proverbs 8:22–31 and other passages in Proverbs 1–9.

> From heaven the peoples are favored;
> Wisdom is of the gods.
> Indeed, she is precious to the gods;
> her kingdom is et[er]nal.
> She has been established by Shamayn;
> yea, the Holy Lord has exalted her.

The nearest biblical text is Sirach 24:4: "I dwelt in the highest heaven, / and my throne was in a pillar of cloud." Also relevant is *1 Enoch* 32:1-2: "Wisdom found no place where she could dwell, and her dwelling was in heaven."

Biblical wisdom literature is thus truly international, being found in the great empires that dominated Israel's world as well as in the geographically closer cities of the Levant. No category of biblical literature is more completely attested outside the Bible than the wisdom literature. It is easy to see why. People find common ground in their personal and familial fears, worries, and hopes.

RECOMMENDED READING

Egypt

Brunner, Helmut. *Die Weisheitsbücher der Ägypter.* Zürich: Artemis, 1991. The best comprehensive treatment, with translations of the instructions and related texts.

Lichtheim, Miriam. *Ancient Egyptian Literature.* 3 vols. Berkeley, Calif.: University of California, 1973–80. The best English translation with brief introduction.

————. *Late Egyptian Wisdom Literature in the International Context.* Orbis Biblicus et Orientalis 52. Göttingen: Vandenhoeck & Ruprecht, 1983.

Simpson, W. Kelly. *The Literature of Ancient Egypt.* 2nd ed. New Haven: Yale, 1973. Selections and brief comment.

Wilson, John. *ANET.* Selections are in pp. 405-10, 412-25, 431-34.

Mesopotamia

Alster, Bendt. *Proverbs of Ancient Sumer: The World's Earliest Proverb Collection.* Bethesda, Md.: CDL, 1997. This is the best English translation and treatment of the Sumerian proverbs.

ANET, 425-27, 435-40, 600-604, for selections in both Akkadian and Sumerian.

Foster, Benjamin R. *Before the Muses: An Anthology of Akkadian Literature.* Two vols. Bethesda, Md.: CDL, 1993.

Lambert, W. G. *Babylonian Wisdom Literature.* Oxford: Clarendon, 1960.

Römer, Willem H. Ph., and Wolfram von Soden. *Weisheitstexte I.* Texte aus der Umwelt des Alten Testaments 3. Gütersloh: Gerd Mohn, 1990.

Canaan

Bergant, Dianne. *Israel's Wisdom Literature.* Minneapolis: Fortress, 1997. A study of all the wisdom books using "the integrity of creation"as the basic interpretive perspective.

Lindenberger, James. "Ahiqar," in *The Old Testament Pseudepigrapha.* Garden City, N.Y.: Doubleday, 1985. Pp. 479-507. See also *ANET,* 427-30.

CHAPTER 3

THE BOOK OF PROVERBS

The book of Proverbs is an anthology of collections and appendixes, which were composed and collected from the earliest days of the monarchy (ca. 1000 B.C.E.) to the end of the sixth century B.C.E. Exile and, in the opinion of many scholars, for several centuries thereafter. The book contains several types, or genres, of literature, but the most common are the aphorism and instruction. Aphorisms are still current; we use proverbs every day (though perhaps less than our grandparents did) to help us come to decisions and to add wit to our speech. Instructions are another matter. In today's world, instructions are the booklets that come with appliances and cars. They show us how to operate computers and tell us how to launder different fabrics, and we throw them aside after we read them. We do not like advice, *especially* when it comes from people who claim to be wiser than we are.

The book of Proverbs means something a bit different by proverb and instruction than we do. Our preferences and biases need not stand in the way of enjoying the book and profiting from its shrewd and often surprising point of view. Why? Essentially, because Proverbs does not provide information. It is not a book of facts. Its "wisdom" is a skill, an art—the art of living well. Its concern is not *what* but *how*.

It is not surprising that many people think of Proverbs as didactic and having a doctrine. Some commentators focus on *what* the sages believed and taught, and reduce their teaching to a system. This approach is relatively modern and Western, a result of the "doctrinalization" of Christianity over the last few centuries that has transposed a way of life expressed in music, ritual, art, and literature, into formulas and statements. Proverbs, however, is concerned not with systems of thought but with living well and enjoying the world as a divine gift.

This chapter is less concerned with Proverbs' doctrines than with helping readers listen to its instructions and ponder its witty sayings. For Proverbs to speak we must allow its rhetoric free play. Rhetoric, needless to say, is positive in this usage: how a piece of literature engages and persuades its audience, how it is eloquent.

The following pages will give essential material on (1) the literary structure and purpose of the book, (2) the genres, (3) the social location, (4) the main assumptions and concepts of Proverbs, and (5) analyses of representative texts in all parts of Proverbs, which are intended as models.

LITERARY STRUCTURE AND PURPOSE

How does the book arrange its parts? Does it organize them in an artistic way or is it merely an archive? How does the book begin and end? Are its parts connected and if so, how? Is there a literary unity and hence one aim for the book?

The size and scope of the book of Proverbs is impressive by ancient Near Eastern standards. Compared with ancient Near Eastern literature, the incorporation into one book of so many different genres (instructions, sayings, riddles, poems) on so large a scale is extraordinarily impressive. By comparison Egyptian instructions seem simple; they have an introduction, exhortations and admonitions with supporting axioms. Proverbs, in contrast, anthologizes instructions, speeches, and collections of sayings into a volume of about 930 lines, about the size of one book of Samuel or the Gospel of Matthew.

Most scholars would agree on the following schematic outline.

43

Is there a principle of unity behind such diversity? The answer lies in the introduction (1:1-7), which makes three important points: the author (and the book's "authority"), its purpose, and the audience it assumes.

The proverbs of Solomon son of David,
    king of Israel:
For learning about wisdom and instruction,
    for understanding words of insight,
for gaining instruction in wise dealing,
    righteousness, justice, and equity;
to teach shrewdness to the simple,
    knowledge and prudence to the young—
let the wise also hear and gain in learning,
    and the discerning acquire skill,
to understand a proverb and a figure,
    the words of the wise and their riddles.
The fear of the LORD is the beginning of knowledge;
    fools despise wisdom and instruction.

Like Egyptian instructions, the book opens with an elaborate title and statement of author, purpose, and benefits to the reader. The first word names the genre, Hebrew *mishlê*, conventionally translated "proverbs," but actually designating more types than just proverbs. It includes, for example, instructions, sayings, poems, and riddles. The second word names the author, Solomon, king of Israel (961–922 B.C.E.), to whom the whole book is attributed. Biblical books (like Egyptian books) do not generally name an author; one kind of book, wisdom literature, is the exception. All the biblical wisdom literature except Job is attributed to King Solomon (Proverbs, Qoheleth, Song of Songs) or makes Solomon a hero and model (Sirach and Wisdom of Solomon). Egyptian instructions were also attributed to kings or highly placed figures. The authority of a wisdom book differed from the authority of a historical chronicle or a liturgical poem in that it came from association with a king whom the gods endowed with skill to govern, or from the maturity and experience of a "senior." Attribution to King Solomon should be interpreted not as a historical statement in a modern sense (though Solomon could have written and collected proverbs) but as a statement of the work's authority (the king endowed with divine wisdom) and literary classification, like the laws of Moses and the psalms of David.

The purpose of the book is stated through the accumulation of synonyms of wisdom rather than differentiating them. The book is concerned with learning (vv. 2-3), with understanding wisdom literature (vv. 2, 6), with teaching (v. 4), and, climactic by position and by reprise of the phrase "wisdom and instruction" from verse 2, with fear of the Lord. An alternative structure is discernible: verse 2a introduces wisdom as a general virtue, which is developed in verses 3-5; verse 2b introduces wisdom as the capacity to interpret learned writings, which is developed in verse 6. Verse 7 is the climax of the introduction, though some translations set the verse apart typographically. The purpose of the book is thus to make its hearers wise, that is, to live successfully, without undue trouble, which means living in "fear of the Lord," revering Yahweh. Another aspect of becoming wise, represented in the alternative structure, is knowing how to read the learned writings (vv. 2a, 6).

Proverbs, like wisdom literature generally in the ancient East, is thoroughly religious. The gods are the creators of the order in the world with which the literature is concerned. Scholarly attempts to argue for an early "secular" stratum of wisdom literature that was supplemented by a later Yahwistic stratum, have not won general acceptance.

The third point in the introduction is the audience. Verse 4 states that the audience is "the simple" and "the young man, boy" *(na'ar)*. The first term is the conventional, all-purpose, English translation of *pĕtî* (fourteen times in Proverbs); it has a range of meaning in the book—inexperienced, untaught, needing instruction, easily seduced, the opposite of wise. Because Proverbs often blends sapiential and ethical categories, "simple" can have a negative connotation and appear in parallel to "fools" (1:32; 8:5) and with "lacking intelligence" (9:4; 16). The second term, "youth, young man," seems to restrict the intended audience to one segment of society, young males. One of the audiences of Proverbs is undoubtedly young men; some instructions compare the quest for wisdom with the quest for a wife or "founding" a household, which in that society seems to have been the task of the young male. He is not, however, the only audience the book envisions. Verse 5 explicitly mentions another—the wise person and the skilled or understanding person. This group is not young, for they have reached a certain level of experience. Proverbs was actually read or heard by people of all kinds; it has in view every Israelite, young and old, skilled and unskilled, male and female. True, some scenes portray young men as actors, but readers of both sexes and all ages may apply the scene to themselves.

GENRES

Another important way the book communicates is through its genres, or types, of literature. Authors speak not in a vacuum but within recognized frameworks of discourse such as novels, plays, short stories, newspaper editorials, sports columns. Readers must know to some extent what to expect, for they need a framework within which to interpret what is said or written. Writers write within conventions; otherwise their readers would have no idea what they say. Writers can follow the conventions, alter them, or even subvert them, but between writer and reader there is a pact or a set of expectations called genre.[1]

The two main categories that will occupy our attention are the instruction and the saying. The instruction is very well represented in Egypt; Helmut Brunner has collected seventeen compositions that range in date from the Old Kingdom in the mid–third millennium to the late–first millennium.[2] Proverbs 22:17–24:22 draws on the *Instruction of Amenemope,* which was originally composed about 1100 B.C.E. In Mesopotamia, the most widely known instruction is the *Instruction of Shuruppak*, composed in Sumerian about the middle of the third millennium, and translated and augmented in subsequent editions. The Kassite scribes of the sixteenth to the twelfth centuries did not copy much Sumerian wisdom literature, so it may be that *Shuruppak* never reached Canaan.

a) *The instructions.* Some of the material in Proverbs 1–9, 22:17–24:22, and 30–31 is instructions like those known in Egypt and Mesopotamia, and it will be useful to briefly characterize this genre of ancient literature, drawing primarily on the more plentiful and relevant Egyptian instances. Other types of literature such as the speeches of Woman Wisdom (1:20-33; chap. 8), numerical poems (6:6-19; 30:11-31), and the encomium on the good wife (31:10-31), will not be dealt with here. First, the chief aim of the instructions is to enable its hearers to live without unnecessary difficulties for themselves.[3] Before everyone there is a path, but there is only one right way, the way of life. The instruction does not hold up to its readers an abstract ideal to live up to but rather mentions many specific cases. Following the behavior depicted in these cases rather than an inner light is what brings success. Order is a societal as well as a natural reality. In Egyptian instructions the order is called *maat*. She is a goddess and can be opposed, but whoever does so can expect punishment sooner or later. The instructions are not about changing society but about a young person adapting to it. In Egypt, the young man advanced himself typically within a *famulus* ("private secretary") system, entering a household as a private secretary. In this milieu, the requirements were discretion, loyalty, and restraint, especially with regard to the women of the household. We will return to these comments on the genre when we examine sample proverbs and instructions.

The genre appears in Proverbs but the biblical authors have added their own emphases such as sharp antitheses between types; they have reduced the amount of exhortation and are less specific. To put it another away, Proverbs emphasizes character rather than acts.

b) *The Saying.* The other main genre represented in Proverbs is the saying or proverb. Examples of sayings in Mesopotamian collections have been given in chapter 2. A good point of departure for the discussion is a widely accepted definition of the proverb: a concise statement of an apparent truth that has currency. "Concise" suggests saturation of thought and artful expression, in sound,

47

wordplay, ellipsis, the employment of irony and paradox. "Apparent" reminds us that a proverb must be "performed," that is, applied to a situation; a proverb is true when it is applied to this case. The last element, "currency," or popular usage, is the one that was probably not true of the bulk of the sayings of Proverbs. Though the point is disputed, it is likely that most were composed by scribes rather than collected from sayings of the people. Unlike those, for example, of the *Oxford Dictionary of English Proverbs,* the extensive proverb collections are not archives of folk sayings. They are rather scribal compositions and constituent parts of the literary whole called the "Proverbs of Solomon."

SOCIAL LOCATION

Who wrote Proverbs? Did professional scribes collect the sayings from the common people and arrange and embellish them? Was Proverbs used in the curriculum of schools in Israel? Who were the original readers?

Unfortunately, there is surprisingly little data about the Palestinian society that created and read the book. We do know that the royal court was the dominant institution for writing and for literature. The king employed scribes to handle correspondence with other nations, to oversee archives and keep records, and to compose literature such as liturgical poetry for the Temple, chronicles, and "wisdom literature" such as Proverbs. The data are few and we are forced to conjecture for some of the answers.

The theories of scholars on the origin of the book can be reduced to two: (1) the instructions and proverbs originated in the tribal society of villages and enshrined family and tribal wisdom; (2) they originated in schools for the upper class or in the royal court. In a word, are the proverbs of tribal or scribal origin?[4] According to the tribal theory, the material in Proverbs, in particular its maxims, arose as oral sayings of simple folk, farmers, artisans, slaves, housewives (though they may have been collected by scribes). Proponents of this view point to the dominance of the family in ancient Israel and the authority of family heads in the society, the everyday topics of the maxims, and the absence of evidence for the alternative postulated source—scribal schools in ancient Israel. The alternative theory is that the material arose among scribes and was perhaps used as school texts.

Unfortunately, there is an absence of compelling evidence for either view. The scribal school is derived by analogy from Egypt, but in Egypt schools were places where young students learned to write by *copying* (not *composing*) wisdom instructions. It was not a school in the sense of an academy or intellectual group. The authors of Egyptian instructions were royal officials writing, it seems, for their own sons (not their pupils) and, through them, for a larger public. As to the evidence for the alternative, a rural and (extended) familial origin, the evidence is likewise not powerful. One cannot argue from Proverbs' topics such as harvesting or the importance of a good name in favor of a village milieu. The topics are sufficiently general to apply to many groups, and can be metaphorical. One can speak "of cabbages and kings" without being a cook or a courtier.

The view taken here is that the Israelite school or family explanation is unlikely as the origin of the material in Proverbs. A scribal origin of some sort cannot be denied. The only solid evidence from Proverbs itself (25:1) tells us that the "men of Hezekiah" (715–687 B.C.E.) collected proverbs of Solomon. Taking this action as typical of the formation of the book, Fox attributes the diversity and unity of the book to the collectors' judgment: "Learned clerks, at least some of them the king's men, were the membrane through which principles, sayings and coinages, folk and otherwise, were filtered. The central collections of Proverbs are their filtrate, an essentially homogeneous one: In the end, it is *their* work and *their* idea of wisdom that we are reading, and it is, not surprisingly, quite coherent."[5] Further evidence of scribal composition is the exceptional artistry of the sayings. The instructions are too indebted to Egyptian models to be attributed to tribal heads. We can conclude, therefore, that the book of Proverbs is an anthology of collections of sayings (some of which were folk in origin) and of instructions. The collectors were most likely scribes employed by the royal court, who were already charged with the creation of literature for temple and court.

MAIN ASSUMPTIONS AND CONCEPTS

Proverbs operates with several assumptions and concepts, not all of which are familiar or fashionable in contemporary Western thinking. It is better not to call them "teachings" or "doctrines," for Proverbs, in my view, did not primarily aim at communicating content. One of its main assumptions can be summed up by Samuel Johnson's dictum in the *Rambler:* "Men more frequently require to be reminded than informed."[6] Proverbs more often invites its readers to look again at what they missed the first time, to view an old reality in a new way. To quote Johnson again, this time his remark on the great eighteenth-century aphorist Alexander Pope: "New things are made familiar, and familiar things are made new."[7] Proverbs invites people into a process, training them to perceive a hitherto hidden dimension to reality. The process is best seen in the sayings. Below we will look at examples, to see how they work to aid the reader to discern and to view afresh.

Proverbs assumes the existence of a world created by God with a certain order or inherent dynamism. People perforce live in God's world, but they do not by that fact know *how to live* in that world. There is much they do not know, much that is hidden. That necessary but hidden knowledge is not data and information, but an order, the way in which the divinely made world operates. To live well, to be "successful," one must know this hidden dimension. The nonapparent world is not easy to attain. One is constantly tempted to miss it and be seduced by "look-alikes." Hence knowledge in Proverbs is not information but a way of seeing reality, a way of conducting oneself, and a way of relating to the order or wisdom that placed one in the world. Note that Proverbs sometimes names God as an agent and at other times simply uses a passive verb to express the way things work, for example, "Plans are foiled for want of counsel, / but succeed with many advisors" (15:22).

Wisdom in Proverbs has a threefold dimension, the sapiential ("a way of seeing reality"), the ethical ("a way of conducting oneself"), and the religious ("a way of relation to the 'order' of God"). The first three sayings in the great collection of 10:1–22:16 illustrate the blend of the three dimensions.

> A wise child makes a glad father,
>   but a foolish child is a mother's grief.
> Treasures gained by wickedness do not profit,
>   but righteousness delivers from death.
> The LORD does not let the righteous go hungry,
>   but he thwarts the craving of the wicked.

Verse 1 is "sapiential," having to do with knowing; it parallels in antithetic lines or cola two sapiential types, the wise and the foolish person. Verse 2 is ethical in its concern that wealth has been unjustly acquired; unjust and just or righteous behavior are contrasted. Verse 3 picks up the righteous and unrighteous contrast from verse 2 but explicitly names Yahweh, the God of Israel, as the guarantor of the divinely implanted system of the world. As Alonso-Schökel has noted,[8] the sayings collection at its very beginning consciously relates the three spheres of knowing, acting, and piety. Proverbs expressly keeps together what elsewhere are separated—knowing, acting, and relating to God or the "ultimate structure of the universe."

These remarks are important for understanding the instructions of Proverbs. The instructions, despite the name, do *not* primarily impart information. Rather, as we shall see in dealing with chapter 2, they generally invite the reader to get in touch with wisdom (1:20-33; chaps. 2, 3, 4, 8 and 9) or unmask seductive alternatives (1:8-19; chaps. 5, 6, 7, 9). The instructions inculcate receptivity to wisdom and vigilance against deception. A central metaphor is trustful relationship, variously, to Wisdom herself, to a teacher, to a father, to both parents, to a wife.

In addition to the assumptions shared with ancient Near Eastern literature, there are several operative concepts in the book. Four can be singled out for comment: (1) its psychology of the human person as a knower and a doer; (2) its use of types, usually antithetically paired, to describe behavior and its consequences; (3) its personification of wisdom as a woman; (4) its dominant metaphor of finding a wife, founding a household.

1) *The psychology of the human person as a knower and doer.* Proverbs makes an extraordinary assumption about the psychological freedom of the human person, but this freedom is balanced by concern with the social implications (on family, community, and God) of human acts. Life is action, and the person is defined through the organs of action—the organs of perception, decision, expression, and motion. Proverbs uses sensory images—eye, ear, mouth (tongue, lips), heart, hands, feet. The book has such confidence in a person's capacity to direct his or her life that it virtually equates knowing the good with doing the good. The ignorance of the fool is not a simple lack of knowledge but an active aversion to it, an aversion arising from cowardice, pride, or laziness. Ignorance has an ethical dimension, and knowing is a moral obligation for human beings. The wise person is morally good; the fool is wicked.

This blending of ethical and sapiential language seems to be an original contribution of the book.

Proverbs 4:20-27 is a good example of a human being as a free and energetic moral agent. The italicized words in my translation designate the organs of perception, decision, or action. By metonymy (cause for effect) the organ stands for the act, for example, eye for sight, foot for walking (= activity).[9]

> My son,[10] pay attention to my words,
>> give your *ear* to my utterances.
> Do not let (them) out of your *eye*sight,
>> hold them in your *heart*,
> for they are life for those who find them,
>> healing for his whole body.
> More than anything you guard, guard your *heart*,
>> for from it comes the source of life.
> Rid yourself of a lying *mouth*;
>> deceitful *lips* keep far from you.
> Keep your *eyes* gazing straight ahead,
>> direct your *eyelids* unswervingly before you.
> Attend to the path of your *feet*
>> so that all your ways turn out well.
> Turn neither to the right nor the left;
>> hold back your *foot* from evil.

The process of learning, deciding, and acting in Proverbs involves perceiving through seeing or hearing, storing the perceptions in the heart, making decisions, and expressing one's heart in words (mouth, lips) and acts (eyes, feet). As in Egyptian instructions, the heart stores and processes data and is best translated by English "mind." The human person is conceived here to be energetic, straining every sense to its limit: one is to "extend" one's ear like an antenna, let nothing escape the eyes, preserve words in the heart, keep false speech away from mouth and lips, hold eyes and eyelids undeviatingly on the goal, keep one's feet from stumbling or taking detours. It is assumed that the disciple is extraordinarily free and available, *disponible* in the French sense. A corollary of Proverbs' presumption of psychological freedom is its contempt toward lazy people, whom it condemns for refusing to act. An example is 26:14: "A door turns on its hinges, / so does a lazy person in bed."

The most important organ in Proverbs is the mouth (or "tongue" and "lips"). Speech is the most important capacity; words are the subject of a large number of proverbs. By speech one defines oneself more completely than in any other act. Through speech, teachers communicate instruction (teaching or discipline), knowledge, and wisdom.[11] Speech must be truthful and reliable; lying is vehemently denounced (17:4; 19:22; 30:6), particularly lying in the law court (6:19; 12:17; 14:5, 25; 19:5, 9, 28; 21:28). A key difference between Woman Wisdom and Woman Folly in chapters 1–9 is the reliability of their words. In a metaphor that holds good in Hebrew as well as English, Wisdom's words are straight, on the level (8:6-11), whereas Folly's are crooked (5:3; 9:17) or smooth and slippery (2:16; 6:24; 7:5).

The emphasis on personal freedom, and the equating of wisdom with virtue and ignorance with malice, are not the whole story, however. Proverbs is keenly aware of the givenness of human life, and expresses that givenness with the metaphor of the way. One's free choice places one on a path or way that has its own dynamic, independent of the agent.[12] By one's choices one ends up walking in "the way of the righteous" (e.g., 2:20; 4:18) or "the way of the wicked" (e.g., 4:14, 19; 12:26; 15:9). Two ways lie before you. Your actions put you on one or the other. Each has its inherent dynamic, toward death or toward life, for God (or the cosmic order) would see to the "completion" of human acts. The concept of the two ways is not static; one can get on and off by one's conduct. One's free choices put one on route, but the route has its own destination. Thus does Proverbs balance personal freedom with its social consequences. In Proverbs' use of the two ways, one joins a community of people on the path and shares their fate, as in the opening scene of 1:8-19.

The most extended treatment of the two ways in Proverbs is 4:10-19.

Hear, my child, and accept my words,
    that the years of your life may be many.
I have taught you the way of wisdom;
    I have led you in the paths of uprightness.
When you walk, your step will not be hampered;
    and if you run, you will not stumble.
Keep hold of instruction; do not let go;
    guard her, for she is your life.
Do not enter the path of the wicked,

and do not walk in the way of evildoers.
Avoid it; do not go on it;
 turn away from it and pass on.
For they cannot sleep unless they have done wrong;
 they are robbed of sleep unless they have made someone stumble.
For they eat the bread of wickedness
 and drink the wine of violence.
But the path of the righteous is like the light of dawn,
 which shines brighter and brighter until full day.
The way of the wicked is like deep darkness;
 they do not know what they stumble over.

Verses 18-19 add to the metaphor of the way the images of light and darkness. The light-dark contrast is a harbinger of later usage, such as the children of darkness and the children of light at Qumran and in the Gospel of John.

2) *The use of types, usually antithetically paired, to describe behavior and its consequences.* Another idea central to Proverbs is its use of character types. The main antithetical characters are the wise and the foolish, the righteous and the wicked, the lazy and the diligent, the rich and the poor. Each set of polarities has its own characteristics; treatments of the wise and the foolish show little interest in retribution with Yahweh as agent, whereas divine retribution is a strong interest with the righteous and wicked. Rich and poor, as noted by a number of recent publications, are related uniquely: "Riches are traced back particularly to the commitment of the rich person, but the wise are well aware that diligence by itself is not responsible; on the other hand, poverty is not solely to be laid at the door of laziness."[13] It is good to remind ourselves that the aphorisms were written not in order to motivate the foolish, wicked, and lazy to change their ways but to motivate the virtuous. The character types are concerned with action, as is shown by the predominance of verbs. The concept of "the way" plays an important role in the full working out of the types.

In addition to these types, persons or groups recur in the book—father-mother-slave-son, friend-neighbor, the king, and the role of the woman. Father-mother-slave-son constitute the household, an institution that is important in Proverbs not only because of the metaphor of founding and maintaining a house established in chapters 1–9, but also because the household is so important in life. The household is viewed from the experience of the male.

3) *The strong personification of wisdom as a woman.* It is not surprising that Proverbs personifies wisdom, for personification is common in the Bible, for example, "O send out your light and your truth; / let them lead me" (Ps 43:3); "Steadfast love and faithfulness will meet; / righteousness and peace will kiss each other" (Ps 85:10). The surprising thing is that the book so persistently focuses on wisdom itself, which differs from the concern of nonbiblical wisdom literature with wise *acts;* the personification is strong and persistent.[14] Wisdom gives long speeches and she has an equally vivid counterpart, Folly. Wisdom's speeches inculcate no particular teaching but urge obedience to her as one who represents Yahweh. Her message is herself.

The personification of wisdom in Proverbs is so distinctive that it has stimulated scholars to search for its origins in other cultures. One scholarly suggestion is that she was originally a Canaanite goddess of wisdom who represents the institution of the school. Another is that she is derived from the Egyptian goddess of wisdom, *Maat.* A third suggestion is that she is a "contrast phenomenon" that was created literarily as an antithesis to Woman Folly. Evidence for the first suggestion is lacking; the second proposal is not compelling, for *Maat* is not strongly personified; she gives no speeches in her own name, for example. The third possibility, that Wisdom was created by Proverbs to be a foil to the "wrong woman," is the most likely theory, in the view taken here. The reason is that Woman Folly has antecedents in earlier literature. There existed stories of seductive women offering a young hero life but ultimately dealing him death: the goddess Ishtar in Gilgamesh, Anat in the Ugaritic Aqhat story, and, in a very transposed form, in the *Odyssey* characters Calypso and Circe. If these seductresses (along with traditional warnings against "foreign women") were models for the seductive woman in Proverbs, then perhaps Woman Wisdom has been created by the author as a contrast. It is important to remember, however, that the origin of Woman Wisdom or Folly is not of primary importance. What is important is the way the women function in the book.[15]

How do the women function in chapters 1–9? Woman Wisdom has two speeches (1:20-33 and chap. 8) and in 9:1-6, 11 she invites passersby to her banquet. The other woman does not have an independent speaking role, appearing only as an object of warning in the teacher's instructions in chapters 2:16-19; 5, 6, and 7. In the matching portraits of two women in chapter 9, they appear together

for the only time in the book. There are other speakers besides
Wisdom in chapters 1–9: the parents in 1:8-19 and 6:20-35; the
father alone in 4:1-9; a teacher in chapter 2; 4:10-19, 20-27; chapter
5; 6:1-19; chapter 7. Who do the women address? According to the
introduction (1:1-7), the audience consists both of "the simple and
youths" (1:4-5) and "the wise" (1:5). Woman Wisdom similarly
addresses all human beings (8:4) but singles out the simple and
youths (8:5). The duality of the audience adds richness. One audience is an inexperienced young man about to leave his parents'
household, find a wife, and found his home (1:8-19), or newly
married and learning to maintain his household. Most readers are
not in that category but can easily apply that liminal situation to
themselves. Our encounter as readers with Woman Wisdom therefore has a context: she addresses all of us at a critical moment in
our lives, when we are, so to speak, in the process of building our
lives, founding a household, seeking a relationship. The book takes
a particular moment in a youth's coming of age and uses it as an
analogy.

4) *The dominant metaphor of finding a wife, founding a household.* The figures of the two women (especially Woman Wisdom)
and the persistent metaphor of finding a wife, or relating properly
to her, and founding a household or maintaining it, provide a lens
for reading chapters 1–9. Chapters 5, 6, and 7 at one level warn a
married man not to commit adultery, because of its high personal
and social costs and because of one's delightful wife. Metaphorically, the warnings are now against allowing seductions of any kind
to disturb the relationship one is invited to have with wisdom.
Wisdom is an attractive woman who invites people into a long-term,
marriagelike relationship with her, which is founded on her truthfulness, bounty, and relationship with Yahweh. Her appeal is to
anyone who wishes to be a companion of wisdom and enjoy the
bounty of those favored by God. The personification of wisdom
makes her active role vis à vis the reader much more vivid.

ANALYSES OF REPRESENTATIVE TEXTS

Having looked at the genres, structure, and ideas of the book,
let's now let the book speak for itself. The rest of the chapter
provides examples of instructions and sayings, which are interesting in themselves and can also serve as models for understanding

similar pieces in Proverbs. I begin with representative instructions of chapters 1–9, then sayings in chapters 10–22 and 25–29, excerpts from the instruction in 22:17–24:22, and I conclude with the poem on the virtuous wife in chapter 31.

Instructions

Three passages are taken from chapters 1–9: (1) the opening instruction of the parents in 1:8-19; (2) the speeches of Woman Wisdom in 1:20-33 and chapter 8; (3) the speech of the teacher in chapter 2; and (4) the warnings against Woman Folly.

1) *The Opening Scene: Leaving Parents and Home.* The opening scene establishes the context of the wisdom instructions or lectures: a young person leaving parents and home to found a house of his own. It establishes the systematic metaphor[16] of an inexperienced ("simple") person making fundamental choices and tempted to depart from traditional values. Metaphor is introduced in this scene and maintained in the rest of the book. There are thus two levels in chapters 1–9. On one level, a young man is warned by parents, father, and teacher against bad companions and against the promiscuity and adultery that will ruin his marriage and household. He is exhorted to seek the right wife or, if he is married, to be faithful to the wife he has. This level is portrayed with typical ancient Eastern features. On the second level, the scene is shifted from its specific setting to a broader context. Any person can apply to himself or herself the situation of achieving maturity, finding a wisdom that is self-constructed but truly "out there," learning to discern the true from the deceptive, learning to establish a household or life. The two levels coexist throughout the book.

The scene-setting opening begins with the parents' voice. In my translation here, repeated Hebrew words are italicized. Verse 16 is secondary and has been omitted; it is not in the best Greek manuscripts and was probably copied from Isaiah 59:7.

> [8]Hear, my son, the instruction of your father,
>   do not disdain the teaching of your mother,
> [9]for they are a handsome diadem for your head
>   and a pendant for your neck.
> [10]My son, if sinners entice you,
>   do not consent, if they say:
> [11]"*Walk* with us,
>   we will *set an ambush* for blood,

lie in wait for the innocent *senselessly.*
¹²We will swallow them alive, like Sheol,
  whole and entire, like those going down to the Pit.
¹³We will obtain all kinds of precious treasure,
  we will fill our houses with the loot.
¹⁴Throw in your lot with us,
  we all have a single purse."
¹⁵My son, do not *walk* on the way with them,
  keep your foot from their path,
¹⁷for *senselessly* would the net be thrown high
  in the sight of a winged creature.
¹⁸As for them, they are *setting an ambush* for their own blood,
  lying in wait for their own lives.
¹⁹Such is the path of everyone greedy for gain;
  it takes the life of its owner.

Several items require comment. The structure is simple: the parents quote the sales pitch of the evil companions (vv. 11-14) and then give their own exhortation for their way of life (vv. 15-19). There are several recurring words or phrases: "senselessly" in verses 11 and 17; "walk" in verses 11 and 15; "set an ambush" and "lie in wait" in verses 11 and 18. The metaphor of the two ways is used; the parents warn not against a particular sin but against a way of life, a group of people, which their son will be invited to join. The parents unmask the deceptive invitation (as the wisdom teachers and Wisdom herself will later do) by showing that the violence of the wicked will come back on themselves. The ambush they set for the innocent senselessly (v. 11) will entrap them (v. 18). A law of retribution operates unseen. Verse 17 has been subject to several interpretations but the following sense is more probable. Since the Hebrew verb for "to throw high" is never used of casting a net to trap prey, "throwing the net high" must mean to lift it up for display. The meaning of the verse is that no hunter ever lifts up the net for the prey to see, but keeps it hidden. So also the law of retribution is hidden from sinners. The passive verb is called a divine passive, which is a reverentially indirect way of stating divine action.

On one level the parents exhort their son to avoid the violence that comes back upon its perpetrator. On another level, we are to understand that life lies before us as a dual path. One places oneself on one of the paths by one's acts, joining others on the path. Each path has inherent consequences. The paradox of the last line is succinct: what is possessed unjustly kills its possessor (cf. 10:2 and 11:4).

2) *The Speeches of Woman Wisdom.* Wisdom's two speeches (1:20-33; chap. 8) are unparalleled in their vivid personification and passion but not easy to understand. On first reading, they seem repetitive and abstract.

The First Speech (1:20-33).[17] Wisdom addresses the inexperienced or "simple" youth, the "implied audience," who also stands for the reader intent on "becoming acquainted with wisdom and instruction" (1:2-7). She speaks to all but focuses on the inexperienced, those not yet wise, who are liable to refuse her. The following translation renders verses 22-23 differently from many translations. The text was confused even before the Greek translation of the second century B.C.E. In brief, the verb rendered "turn away" below was understood by many in the opposite sense, "to turn toward, to heed," and a stray couplet ("[How long] will scorners join in scorning, will fools hate knowledge") was added to the verse. It is omitted here.

> [20]Wisdom cries aloud in the bazaar,
>   in the squares she lifts up her voice,
> [21]at the head of the bustling street she calls,
>   at the entrance of the gate,
>   in the city she speaks her message:
> [22]"How long, simple ones, will you go on loving ignorance,
> [23]   will you turn away from my reproof?
>   Let me now pour out my thoughts to you,
>   speak my words to you."

The tone is harsh and accusatory. We soon learn the reason: the youth has a history of ignoring her instruction (vv. 24-31). The shift from second person (vv. 24-27) to third person (vv. 28-31) is normal in Hebrew style and is not evidence for two different authors. Despite her reproving tone, Wisdom does not threaten her hearers with any punishment beyond the consequences of their own wicked behavior. She will laugh when the inevitable disaster comes (vv. 26-27) and will simply not be there (v. 28).

She sums up her message and ends with a loving invitation, which contrasts with the previous harshness.

> Yes, the turning away of the untaught will kill them,
>   the self-sufficiency of fools will destroy them.

59

But the person who listens to me will dwell secure,
  will be at rest, free from the fear of disaster. (my translation)

The Second Speech (chap. 8). Wisdom's great speech reverses the extended threat plus a one-line promise of her first speech with an extended promise-invitation plus a one-line threat in v. 36. All is promise with only the last verse containing a threat. She stands in the same place, the upper part of the city where government and business was carried on, speaking to all but focusing on the inexperienced, the not-yet wise. The poem is in four sections:

I. 1. vv. 1-5	2. vv. 6-10	III. 1. vv. 22-26	2. vv. 27-31
II. 1. vv. 12-16	2. vv. 17-21	IV. vv. 32-36	

  ⁵O simple ones, learn prudence;
    acquire intelligence, you who lack it.
  Hear, for I will speak noble things,
    and from my lips will come what is right;
  for my mouth will utter truth;
    wickedness is an abomination to my lips.
  All the words of my mouth are righteous;
    there is nothing twisted or crooked in them.
  They are all straight to one who understands
    and right to those who find knowledge.
  ¹⁰Take my instruction instead of silver,
    and knowledge rather than choice gold.

Wisdom gives no advice and is remarkably vague. She asks her hearers to trust and believe *her;* she seeks a relationship to her disciple. In verses 12-21 she promises to give her devotee the art of governing and the traditional benefits of wisdom—prosperity, wealth, and long life.

In the history of interpretation, the most influential part of the poem is section III, verses 22-31, where Wisdom tells about her role in Yahweh's creating the world.

  The Lord created me at the beginning of his work,
    the first of his acts long ago.
  Ages ago I was set up,
    at the first, before the beginning of the earth.
  When there were no depths I was brought forth,
    when there were no springs abounding with water.

Before the mountains had been shaped,
    before the hills, I was brought forth—
when he had not yet made earth and fields,
    or the world's first bits of sod.
When he established the heavens, I was there,
    when he drew a circle on the face of the deep,
when he made firm the skies above,
    when he established the fountains of the deep,
when he assigned to the sea its limit,
    so that the waters might not transgress his command,
    when he marked out the foundations of the earth,
then I was beside him, like a master worker;
    and I was daily his delight,
    rejoicing before him always,
rejoicing in his inhabited world
    and delighting in the human race.

This section grounds Wisdom's authority. Why should a disciple trust and believe her? The reason: Wisdom was created before anything else, which is a mark of the highest honor. This section has two parts, part 1 emphasizing the birth of Wisdom *prior* to all else; part 2 stating she was *with Yahweh* during the creation. The word translated "master worker" (*'āmôn*) is controverted. In antiquity it was interpreted either as "darling, child" or "worker, arranger," the latter ultimately derived from Akkadian *ummānu*, "sage, artisan." The Akkadian term is used in a mythological sense for the venerable sages who lived after the great flood of Mesopotamian lore; they brought the human race culture and specialized knowledge. Chapter 8 applies the term to Wisdom, who is a heavenly being giving beneficial knowledge to the human race. In the chapter, Wisdom is a sage and a woman seeking disciples. The important point is that Wisdom establishes her authority: the reason she is to be trusted by her hearers is her relationship with Yahweh. In fact, the relationship she wishes with her discipleship is modeled on her relationship with Yahweh.

    I was daily his *delight,*
      rejoicing before him always,
    rejoicing in his inhabited world
      and *delighting* in the human race. (italics added)

The poem ends (vv. 32-36) with an appeal to the disciple to wait at

Wisdom's door as a loving disciple. Love language is used, underscoring Wisdom's desire for disciples.

Chapter 8 became the most famous chapter in Proverbs. Ben Sira about 190 B.C.E. imitated its thirty-five-line structure in Sirach 24, and reprised 8:22 in 24:9, "Before the ages, in the beginning, he created me." In Sirach, Wisdom leaves her heavenly home and finds a new dwelling in Jerusalem, where she is to be found "in the book of the covenant of the Most High God, the law that Moses commands us" (v. 23). Jewish tradition follows Sirach in associating and identifying Wisdom with the Torah. In the New Testament, the first chapter of the Gospel of John alludes to Proverbs 8:22, "In the beginning was the Word, and the Word was with God, and the Word was God" (1:1). John combines into one term "the Word" (Greek *logos*) from Genesis 1 ("Then God *spoke,* 'Let there be . . . .' ") and wisdom from Proverbs 8.

3) *Instruction on Wisdom (chap. 2).* Chapter 2 is a poem in twenty-two lines, which is the number of consonants in the Hebrew alphabet. In most acrostic poems, successive letters of the alphabet begin each line as in 31:10-31, but the form is modified here: the first Hebrew letter '*āleph* begins several key lines in part 1 (vv. 1, 4, 5, 9) and the middle letter *lāmed* begins several key lines in part 2 (vv. 12, 16, 20). The poem invites the reader to a way of life: strive after wisdom with every nerve (vv. 1-4) and Yahweh will give it to you, including his presence and protection on your way (vv. 5-8); wisdom will come to you (vv. 8-11) and protect you from wicked men (vv. 12-16) and a particular kind of woman (16-19) with the result that you will walk on the way of the good and enjoy the bounty promised to them (vv. 20-22). The poem invites its hearer into a paradox: *strive* with all *your* might for wisdom so that *God* may *give* it to you.

The poem introduces us to the "foreign woman," who appears in chapters 5, 6, 7, and 9. The foreign (or "wrong woman") comes from Egyptian instructions. For example, the Instruction of Any (written between 1550–1300 B.C.E.), exhorts: "Beware of a woman who is a stranger, / One not known in her town: Don't stare at her when she goes by, / Do not know her carnally. . . . She is ready to ensnare you, / A great deadly crime when it is heard." The figure here is metaphorical; her seductive words can lead to death, the opposite of the life that Yahweh and wisdom give.

The poem is an invitation to a relationship with wisdom itself rather than an exhortation to perform wise actions. Seeking wisdom itself brings one before God, who bestows wisdom and protection from the real danger posed by wicked people and especially by seductive words. Note the use of words beginning with 'āleph and lāmed and the artistic structure. The words beginning with 'āleph and lāmed are italicized.

Part 1 (vv. 1-11). (v. 1) '*im* = *if* you accept my words . . . (v. 3) '*im* = *if* you cry out to understanding . . . (v. 4) '*im* = *if* you seek it like silver . . . (v. 5) '*āz* = *then* you will understand . . . (v. 9) '*āz* = *then* you will understand . . .

Part 2 (vv. 12-22). (v. 12) *lāmed* = *to* save you from an evil way . . . (v. 16) *lāmed* = *to* save you from the foreign woman . . . (v. 20) *lāmed* = *so that you* may walk on the way of the good . . .

One can see how words of the poem elicit in the reader a desire for the virtue of wisdom. The poem forms character.

4) *Warnings Against Woman Folly: chapters 5; 6:20-35; 7.* These three exhortations, or admonitions, are addressed primarily to young married men. Chapter 7 does not say explicitly that the youth is married, but the woman certainly is. What is warned against is adultery, violating the marital relationship. The introductory chapters of Proverbs introduced the metaphorical level, which makes this very specific situation applicable to all readers. Stay with wisdom; beware of deceptive substitutes.

In the warnings, there are three characters: Wisdom, the youth, and the "foreign" or "wrong" woman. The wrong woman offers excitement to the young man, but her offer is spurious, for death results from her words. There is no need to analyze the three exhortations in detail, for they are straightforward exhortations to remain faithful to the marriage bond. For the most part, the motives given are practical. Virtue keeps one out of trouble and makes one happy; in short, it gives "life."

To summarize the chief points of chapters 1–9, first, Wisdom itself can be grasped but it is also a gift. That great paradox generates much of the paradox in the individual sayings in chapters 10–31. Because God's justice operates in a hidden manner in the world, an exclusively literal approach to describing life is not sufficient. Second, wisdom is personified as a woman and speaks within a scenario that includes another woman. The scenario has erotic and linguistic aspects; that is, hearers are invited into a long-term relationship with wisdom and warned against entering into a relationship with the other woman; they are to discern the real meaning of the woman's words. Hence discernment is called for, and the presence of irony must be taken into account. Last, finding a spouse can also be seen as founding a house(hold), as choosing in the defining moment as one leaves one's parental house in order to found one's own.

A final question must be asked, and the question provides a transition to the next section. What is the life Woman Wisdom offers? As in other passages in the Bible (e.g., Genesis 2–3; Ps 27:4; 84:4), life is not mere biological life but life *with another.* To live, therefore, means to live *with* Wisdom, to banquet with her in her house. According to 9:4, it is the opposite of living in "simpleness" or ignorance. Living with Wisdom means pondering the wisdom sayings of chapters 10–22 and 25–29, and to that section we now turn.

Sayings

Most of the sayings are in chapters 10:1–22:16 and 25–29. The two collections (totaling 512 aphorisms) describe themselves as "proverbs of Solomon" (10:1 and 25:1). The meaning of many of them is not obvious. Unlike most modern proverbs, they require pondering. That pondering is perhaps what it means to live with wisdom, to live in her house. Just as one must reflect on a saying, so one must reflect on the events of one's life. To take the measure of these wise words teaches one to take the measure of life. They are a school of discernment. Examples of sayings follow. Modern translations vary in their sensitivity to wordplay, paradox, and the general wit of the sayings. Again, in addition to the NRSV, the two English translations I recommend are the *New American Bible (NAB)* and *Tanakh,* the Jewish Publication Society version. The translations given here are all my own, designed to bring out wordplay and wit.

1. 10:1: A wise son makes his father rejoice, / but a foolish son is his mother's heartache.

"Wise" means not so much intelligence but the art of leading a good life, which yields blessings to oneself and one's family. Children's wisdom or folly has consequences for children and parents, and, further, advertises to the world the quality of their parents. This antithetical proverb has three contrasts: father and mother, wise and foolish, joy and grief.

This verse is programmatic in the structure of the book. The characters, "son," "father," and "mother," point back to the opening line of the instruction in 1:18: "Hear, my *son*, the instruction of your *father*; do not disdain the teaching of your *mother*." The son (= disciple) was the object of parental exhortation in chapters 1–9. Founding or maintaining a house is an important theme of those chapters. The verse points forward in the book as the first of many sentences on domestic happiness or unhappiness in family relationships—between father and son (15:20; 17:21, 25; 19:13, 26; 23:22-25) and between husband and wife. Like a red thread through the collection, the domestic sayings keep before the reader the metaphor of the house(hold). As noted, this verse, and the next two, introduce the reader to the ranges of wisdom—the sapiential (v. 1), the ethical (v. 2), and the religious (v. 3).

2. 17:9: Whoever seeks friendship conceals an offense, / but whoever repeats a story separates friends.

The saying states a paradox: one finds by concealing and loses by revealing. To find love or friendship, overlook ("conceal") the offenses of the other, exercise restraint and forgiveness. To complete the antithesis, 9b tells how to lose a friend—just reveal a slander.

3. 21:23: Who guards his mouth and his tongue, / guards himself from troubles.

Wordplay is important in many of the sayings. The wordplay is on the two senses of the verb *šāmar*, "to guard, control" and "to guard, protect." There is a further wordplay on the range of meanings of *nepeš*, which is literally the throat area, the moist and breathing center of the body. By metonymy it is "life, self, soul." If you guard (= control) your tongue you guard (= protect) your "throat," your center, your life. To guard your "throat area" (= life) guard your throat-tongue (= words).

4. 18:23: The poor person must say "please," / but the wealthy person can give a rude response.

This saying is an observation, a subtype of saying, which gives an experience of life seemingly without comment, though often with an implicit judgment. Many of the statements about rich and poor in Proverbs are in the form of observations (10:15; 13:7, 8, 23; 14:20; 19:4, 7; 22:7; 28:15).[18] This verse states concretely the situation of the poor, their powerlessness and need to ingratiate themselves with others. The wealthy, in contrast, can speak as they please.

> 5. 9: A thorn attaches to the hand of a drunkard / and a proverb to the mouth of a fool.

The proverb is an example of Proverbs' humor, which is often sardonic. A proverb is not a byte of information but must be applied wisely to a specific situation. A proverb must be performed. Fools may quote them, but they do not have the wisdom or practical skill to apply them rightly. Their proverbs are like thorns, which one finds on one's clothing and cannot explain how they got there.

Most of the humor in the book is at the expense of the lazy. Proverbs regards the sluggard with derision, chiefly because the type does not rise to situations that call for action. Proverbs' ideal is the self-actualizing person, someone who uses heart, lips, hands, feet to keep to the good path. How ridiculous is the statement of the sluggard, "There's a lion in the road, / there's a lion in the square!" (26:13). To quote them is to condemn them. Another memorable picture is 26:14: "The door turns on its hinges, / the sluggard, on his bed!" The sluggard can no more rise from bed than a door can leave its hinges.

These examples provide only a hint of the wit and challenge of the many sayings. Readers who do not read Hebrew may need to look at several translations.

An Adapted Egyptian Instruction: 22:17–24:22: The Words of the Wise. Since the publication of the Egyptian *Instruction of Amenemope* in 1924, scholars have recognized that this section of Proverbs draws upon the Egyptian work, which was written ca. 1200 B.C.E. The genre of instructions has already been discussed under "Genre," so we limit ourselves to a single interesting text, 23:1-3:

> When you sit down to dine with a ruler,
>   consider carefully what is before you;
> And stick the knife in your jaw
>   if you have a big appetite.
> Do not desire his viands,
>   for it is a food that deceives. (my translation)

Luxurious meals apparently were rare enough to be occasions of intemperance for young courtiers with an appetite for food, wine— and higher social position. The Old Egyptian *Instruction of Ptahhotep* urges self-control: "When you are a guest / at the table of one who is greater than you / then take what he gives you, as they serve it before you. / Do not look at what lies before *him,* but always look only at what lies before *you.*"[19] *Amenemope* chapter 23: "Do not eat in the presence of an official / And then set your mouth before him; / If you are sated pretend to chew, / Content yourself with your saliva. / Look at the bowl that is before you, / And let it serve your needs. An official is great in his office, / As a well is rich in drawings of water" (13-20). The Proverbs passage goes beyond the table etiquette proposed by the Egyptian instructions to expose the folly of the social ploy itself. The phrase "set before you" refers both to food and host and has the meaning: Consider carefully the food and host before you and put your knife not to your food to satisfy your hunger but to your jaws to restrain your hunger. In the end, you will obtain neither food nor favor.

Encomium on the Capable Wife: 31:10-31. The Poem on the Valiant Wife is an acrostic poem of twenty-two lines (cf. chap. 2), in which each line begins with a letter of the Hebrew alphabet. The wife is described by her activity; she runs an enormous and productive household, which provides for her husband all manner of wealth, public repute, children—in short, "life" in the forms that life was presented in Proverbs. The poem has been taken in a variety of ways, as an encomium of woman correcting the book's allegedly negative portrait of women, or as an imitation of the encomia of women found in Egyptian monuments. The most likely interpretation of the poem in its present context is as an illustration of what happens to the man who marries Woman Wisdom. Chapter 9 showed us Woman Wisdom inviting the youth to a banquet, to be with her and imbibe her wisdom. Are we to believe that pondering the sayings that followed chapter 9 are what it means to live with Wisdom, allowing those proverbs to reshape our life? The final poem shows us the youth who has become a friend and disciple of Wisdom: he has found long life, health, repute, children, and domestic happiness. He, and we, now sing the praises of Wisdom who has given all gifts along with her presence.

Her children rise up and call her happy;
    her husband too, and he praises her:
"Many women have done excellently,

but you surpass them all."
Charm is deceitful, and beauty is vain,
    but a woman who fears the LORD is to be praised.
Give her a share in the fruit of her hands,
    and let her works praise her in the city gates.

RECOMMENDED READING

Commentaries

Cohen, A. *Proverbs*. Revised by A. J. Rosenberg. London: Soncino, 1985. Useful summary of much Jewish interpretation.

Delitzsch, Franz. *Proverbs*. Grand Rapids: Eerdmans, 1993. Reprint of 1873 original. Never superseded in its careful, conservative treatment of the masoretic text.

Mckane, W. *Proverbs: A New Approach*. Old Testament Library. 2nd ed. Philadelphia: Westminster, 1977. Excellent linguistic and historical discussion.

Toy, Crawford C. *Proverbs*. International Critical Commentary. New York: Scribners, 1899. Technical and thorough on linguistic details.

Van Leeuwen, Raymond C. "The Book of Proverbs," in *The New Interpreter's Bible*. Vol. 5. Nashville: Abingdon Press, 1997. Pp. 17-264. Carefully done, with attention both to form and meaning, the literary and theological.

Whybray, R. N. *Proverbs*. New Century Bible Commentary. Grand Rapids: Eerdmans, 1994. Presents alternatives, judicious.

Studies

Boström, L. *The God of the Sages: The Portrayal of God in the Book of Proverbs*. Coniectanea Biblica, OT Series 29; Stockholm, 1990.

Bryce, Glendon E. *A Legacy of Wisdom: The Egyptian Contribution to the Wisdom of Israel*. Lewisburg: Bucknell, 1979.

Camp, Claudia V. *Wisdom and the Feminine in the Book of Proverbs*. Sheffield: Almond Press, 1985. A well-informed and perceptive reading.

McCreesh, Thomas P. *Biblical Sound and Sense: Poetic Sound Patterns in Proverbs 1029*. Journal for the Study of the Old Testament Supplement Series 128. Sheffield: Sheffield Academic Press, 1991.

Perry, T. A. *Wisdom Literature and the Structure of Proverbs*. University Park: Pennsylvania State University Press, 1993. A study of the quadripartite structure of individual proverbs.

CHAPTER 4

THE BOOK OF
JOB

Wisdom literature is personal, reflective, and didactic. It is about personal rather than national affairs; it ponders problems and quandaries; it hands on its reflections to others. In the book of Proverbs, the personal and the didactic aspects predominate. In Job, the reflective side is paramount. Job ponders what we today call "the problem of evil" in a typically ancient way, treating evil not abstractly but as embodied in the story of a human being. The book is not unique in refusing to abstract an idea from its instantiation; the biblical psalms of lament see innocence and malice in the form of innocent or malicious human beings. The book of Job discusses divine irrationality and injustice in their effects upon a particular man, Job.

COMPARABLE ANCIENT NEAR
EASTERN LITERATURE

Are there comparable "reflective" and problem-oriented ancient works that might help us to read Job? As noted in the chapter on ancient Near Eastern wisdom literature, it is very helpful to understand the ancient perspective on "wisdom" themes and the literary genres in which they are found. We must know the general to understand the particular.

Egyptian literature has "reflective" works such as *The Dispute Between a Man and His Ba,* in which a man discusses with his soul why he should go on living, given the miseries of life. His *ba* tries to persuade him to remain alive by giving him reasons for hope.[1] Other Egyptian works record social disorder and personal distress with great honesty, but none defend someone's personal honor and innocence with the vehemence of Job.

Mesopotamian literature is more promising. Three works are usually mentioned as comparable to Job: the "Sumerian Job" (= *A Man and His God*), *I Will Praise the Lord of Wisdom* (often cited by its opening words in Akkadian, *Ludlul bēl nēmeqi*), and *The Babylonian Theodicy.* The "Sumerian Job,"[2] was once wise and wealthy and has become poor and victimized. He complains of his misery but persists in prayer, and his personal god turns his suffering into joy. Three points are noteworthy: (1) the god is the man's "personal god," a kind of good angel to an individual and family head, a divine father who begot one, to whom one can bare one's soul, who represents one's interests in the divine assembly, for the high gods were too important to be interested; (2) the Sumerian Job does not argue with the gods but, with exemplary piety, persists in prayer by lamenting and wailing; (3) the man's words ("You [God] have doled out to me suffering ever anew" [line 30]; "Never has a sinless child been born to its mother" [line 103]), illustrate the common belief that the gods who planned the world and its civilization also planned evil and violence; the list of *me*'s (the divine rules for the world) contained not only "truth" and "justice," but also "falsehood" and "lamentation."

Ludlul bēl nēmeqi[3] is less relevant to Job than has sometimes been assumed. Recent publication of the text of tablet I shows that the work is a hymn, informed by profound piety, celebrating the god Marduk who has spurned and then rescued the pray-er. The work shows the extension of Marduk's cosmic role into the domain of the individual. Its solution is one of the heart rather than of the head: instead of wisdom, belief; instead of reason, prayer and adoration. It is not a serious inquiry into the problem of suffering.[4]

The Babylonian Theodicy on the other hand, is very relevant.[5] The work is a dialogue in twenty-seven stanzas (eleven for each

70

speaker) between a sufferer and a sage to whom he goes for comfort and wisdom. About nineteen stanzas are legible, with the best preserved material at the beginning and at the end. Its many manuscripts show the text was widely read. The work is dated by W. G. Lambert to ca. 1000 B.C.E., and by W. von Soden to 800–750 B.C.E. Alone of the ancient texts, *The Babylonian Theodicy* seems to have influenced Job. In stanza 1, the sufferer praises the sage in exalted language ("Who is he whose knowledge could rival yours?") and complains of being the youngest son whose parents have died. The sage replies icily (stanza 2): you speak foolishly; everyone dies; get a protector and pray to your god. The sufferer seeks comfort and emotional support (stanza 3): "Hearken to me but for a moment, hear my declaration." The sage in response accuses the sufferer of being scatterbrained and again tells him to seek god (stanza 4). In stanzas 5–7, the sufferer complains of injustice in the human and animal realms and declares, "(My) god decreed (for me) poverty instead of wealth [stanza 7]." The sage rebukes him sarcastically, "O just, knowledgeable one, your logic is perverse. You have cast off justice, you have scorned divine favor.... The strategy of a god is [as remote as] innermost heaven." The sufferer explodes in anger, "I will ignore (my) god's regulation, [I will] trample on his rites." The stanzas, now fragmentary or even illegible, continue: the sufferer's denial of justice is met by the sage's denunciation of his temerity. Stanza 26 is a turning point: the sage comes to admit the truth of the sufferer's remarks: "Enlil . . . Ea . . . Mami gave twisted words to the human race, They endowed them in perpetuity with lies and falsehood. . . . They bring him to a horrible end, they snuff him out like an ember." The sage admits the gods have put evil in the world. Having won at last the sympathy of the sage, the sufferer acknowledges that he himself is a humble suppliant, and concludes with a prayer, "May the god who has cast me off grant help, May the goddess who has [forsaken me] take pity."

The sage in the *Theodicy* has drawn on traditional thinking about human suffering, but the treasury of ancient Near Eastern thinking on the topic is even larger. William Moran summarizes it.

> In the Old Babylonian period [religious explanation of suffering] may find expression in a simple confession of bewilderment and igno-rance of what one has done, or in the acceptance of one's sinfulness, along with its necessary consequences, as another manifestation of

fragilitas humana common to all men. Later, one may infer from a clear conscience and a life re-examined and found, according to the known rules, faultless, that the gods hold men to the observance of other rules that he cannot know. To these thoughts one may join a contempt for man as the minion of many moods, a creature that may live gloriously only to die miserably. Or one may make the problem of the mind a problem of the heart, and solve it with reasons of the heart. Instead of wisdom, belief; instead of reflection and argument, a hymn to paradox and contradiction. *Credo quia absurdum.* Attitudes and expression change; the theology does not.[6]

A Man and His God (Sumerian Job) accepted human sinfulness and emphasized human fragility. The sage in the *Theodicy* underlined human inability to know the gods' mind. *Ludlul* makes the problem of the mind a problem of the heart: trust in the god (Marduk), whose ways are inscrutable, who puts down only to exalt.

Of the three literary works, *The Babylonian Theodicy* is certainly the most important for Job. How does it help us to understand Job? First, it poses the problem of evil in a *personal* way—it is the speaker who is suffering! He is bereft of normal human support: he is an orphan, the youngest son probably without a legacy (stanza 1), poor and unhappy (stanza 3), aware that society is unjust and incoherent. He is not a disinterested spectator. Second, the sufferer seeks not only counsel but friendship and solace from the sage. He addresses him throughout with respectful titles (possibly, some are sarcastic). There is an ironic tension between the sage's advice to seek solace from the gods and his own unwillingness to give solace. Significantly, it is only when the sage concedes the truth of the sufferer's observations that the sufferer ends his complaints and makes his acknowledgment. Third, the sufferer refuses to give up his perception that his lot is miserable and society is corrupt. Rather, it is the sage who changes, conceding in stanza 26 that the sufferer is right: the gods gave twisted words to the human race and cause the race to suffer every evil. Fourth, from a formal point of view the dialogue is a drama, a conversation between two men that has a beginning, a middle (unfortunately damaged), and an end in which the dramatic tension is resolved.

The *Theodicy* enables us, therefore, to get a feel for the genre of Job, a dramatic dialogue between a sufferer and a sage-friend on the subject of divine justice, which is triggered by the actual suffering of one interlocutor. The personal relationship between sage and sufferer is highly important. The language of address is respectful and self-deprecating in the best tradition of ancient Near Eastern rhetoric, but (at least from the side of the sage) it can be brutal.

Though they share a common genre, the two works are unique realizations of it and are different works. The most important of the differences is stated by Moran: "An explicit, unyielding declaration of innocence is not found before the book of Job."[7] Before Job, the instinctive cry of an afflicted person in the ancient Near East was "What have I done wrong?" The Bible's confession of one God, all-wise and all-powerful, makes its exploration of the problem of evil and of the righteous sufferer more pressing and more poignant than those of its neighbors. For who but the *one* God of Israel is ultimately responsible for *everything* that happens in the world? A second difference is the active presence of God in Job. God initiates the entire drama in chapters 1–2 and concludes it in chapter 42. A third difference is formal: the book of Job is more richly textured with three (four, counting Elihu) sages, is much longer, more varied in style, and freer in composition.

THE DATE AND SOCIAL LOCATION

Having noted the literary genre of Job, we now turn to its social location. Who was the author of Job? When was it written? What issues stirred the author to write? What "interests" or agenda does the book represent and promote? These are all worthwhile questions and are of great contemporary interest. Unfortunately, none can be answered with much certainty.

The book of Job, like most biblical (and ancient Near Eastern) books, is anonymous. Its date of composition is unknown, with scholarly estimates falling between the seventh and the fourth centuries B.C.E. The book contains no allusions to any historical event; its language cannot be fitted easily into any scheme of the history of Hebrew; its ideas are age-old and cannot be dated. Slight support for a preexilic date may be its lack of any allusion to the traumas of the exile when such an association would naturally suggest itself. Its hero is an Edomite, which would be strange after the exile when Edomites were regarded with hostility for taking advantage of Israel. There is a slight probability therefore in favor of the seventh century B.C.E.

Given the uncertainties surrounding authorship and date, little

73

can be said about class interests apart from analyzing the book. The question of the authorship of wisdom literature generally is controverted—was it of scribal or tribal origin?—and the data to resolve the questions are few and indirect. More than is the case with Proverbs, scholars are willing to concede that the author was a learned scribe or clerk familiar with some ancient Near Eastern literature. He appears to have known *The Babylonian Theodicy* among others. Details of his thinking will come out in the course of our analysis.

SCHOLARLY APPROACHES

The goal here is to assist readers as they face the book. That suggests a literary approach in preference to, say, a history-of-ideas focus on theological themes such as suffering or divine justice. The decision to read the text as a literary whole requires decisions about several controverted issues in Job. These are: (1) the relation of the prose prologue (chaps. 1 and 2) and epilogue (42:7-17) to the poetic dialogues (3:1–42:6); (2) the originality and function of chapter 28, the poem on the place of wisdom; (3) the originality and function of chapters 32–37, the speeches of Elihu, the fourth friend; (4) the original order and attribution of the speeches in chapters 22–27, which are now somewhat disturbed. With regard to (1), this book will treat chapters 1–42 as a single literary work. Though many scholars, on the assumption that the prologue and epilogue are later additions, divide the work into two sections, "Job the patient" and "Job the impatient," there is little evidence for such a division.[8] There are, in fact, cross-references between the prose and the poetry. With regard to (2), though the debate on the originality of chapter 28 cannot be decisively resolved, the chapter plays an important role in the narrative. With regard to the Elihu speeches (3), most judge them to be a supplement, the earliest interpretation of the book, but I take them as part of the original narrative. The last point of contention, the proper order of the third cycle of speeches (4), is a more technical problem that can be dealt with in the course of our exposition.

Perhaps the most important assumption for the proper interpretation of Job is that the book is a narrative, a drama with a beginning, middle, and end, with characters, tensions, and resolutions. Though modern readers often want to cut to the chase, focusing immediately on the book's grand ideas such as divine justice and the meaning of suffering, the author of Job carefully and with a sure sense of pacing tells the complicated story of a sufferer, his three sage-friends, and God. The author loved words, reveled in complicated arguments, and was in no hurry to conclude. Unless the reader has a similar love and lots of patience, the book will be merely a backdrop to the discussion of modern questions, an occasion not a cause.

THE BOOK

Whatever "point" the book may make, it makes it through *narrative*, requiring the reader to pay close attention to the story, the beginning, middle, and end. Our first task is to describe the plot.

THE PROLOGUE (CHAPTERS 1–2)

Chapters 1–2 introduce the characters and present the first scene of the drama. The reader meets the *characters:* Job and his family, God, the satan, and the three friends. The satan is a literal translation of the Hebrew word *haśśāṭān* and is not Satan the devil of later times, but a member of the heavenly assembly (cf. 1 Kgs 22:19-23; Isaiah 6). His task evidently is to inquire into the behavior of the human race and to bring back word to God. The very first section, 1:1-5, has as its purpose to characterize Job as just and God-revering; Job's uprightness is revealed by the blessings of children and wealth given him, his peaceful family life, and his concern even for potential sin by members of his family. Characterization ("It was the *custom* of his sons . . ."; "Job *would* send word . . .") shifts to narrative time ("one day," 1:6, 13; 2:1; "then," understood in 1:20; 2:7, 9). A good entry into the *drama* is to look at its opening scenes as two parallel scenarios:

Introduction of Job as a just man

I.	II.
1. Meeting of heavenly court (1:6-12)	1. Meeting of heavenly court (2:1-6)
Does Job not have good reason to revere God?	People will give anything to save their lives.
Permission to touch all he has.	Permission to touch Job.
2. Destruction of Job's wealth and children (1:13-19)	2. Affliction of Job's person (2:7-8)
3. Job's submission (1:20-22)	3. Job's submission (2:9-10)

Arrival and mourning of three friends (2:11-13)

75

The opening verses paint an idyllic picture: a venerable patriarch enjoying every blessing, revering God in exemplary fashion. But Yahweh, the God whom Job reveres ("fears"), acts within a heavenly world Job knows nothing about. The drama begins not with Job but with Yahweh and, in particular, with the satan's question: "Does Job fear God for nothing?" In other words, is Job's vaunted loyalty simply a transaction, a *quid pro quo* arrangement without genuine loyalty to Yahweh? Yahweh accepts the challenge and permits the testing of Job in the form of the destruction of his animals, servants, and children. Job submits without question: "Naked I came from my mother's womb, and naked shall I return there; the LORD gave, and the LORD has taken away; blessed be the name of the LORD."

The next ten verses (2:1-10) are meant to be seen as parallel to 1:6-22, as can be seen by looking at the chart. Parallelism is of great significance in Hebrew rhetoric, for ancient readers and public speakers were evidently able to hold sections in their memory long enough to compare and contrast verses and even the long sections themselves. Small-scale parallelism (of two-line verses) is familiar enough, but there are many large-scale parallelisms, the figures of Woman Wisdom and Woman Folly in Proverbs 1-9, the parallel narratives of Moses' call in Exodus (2:23-6:1 and 6:2-7:7), and some speeches of Deutero-Isaiah. Job 2:1-10 invites the reader to compare and contrast 1:6-22. The stakes are higher here—not Job's property but Job himself! Others are brought into it (Job's wife). Job submits but in different words and with a different assessment by the narrator. Job's three friends learn of his misfortune and now gather around the disfigured hero, remaining with him seven days in a majestic silent tableau. Thus does the dramatic movement of Job begin.

Several details in the prologue require comment. First, Job is in the land of Uz, not precisely locatable but in "the East," which is appropriate for the homeland of a legendary hero. Job is in the class of Noah and Daniel (see Ezek 14:14, 20), who were protagonists of ancient sagas. His legendary righteousness is the important thing, not the fact he is a foreigner. Second, the detailed characterization of God (through his words to the satan) is unusual in the Bible, which generally stays clear of direct description of the deity. God is enthusiastically proud of Job's upright service to him (Job's "fear" in our terms is something like revering God). The reader learns that God's concern is not primarily Job's prosperity or safety but the results of the testing. Thereafter God does not speak until the storm theophany of 38:1. Is there a relationship between the portrait of God here and the portrait of God in the storm speeches? Is God's primary interest in his own wager with the satan a harbinger perhaps of his later reaffirmation that the world is *theo*centric rather than *anthropo*centric? Third, the reader knows what Job and his friends do not, that God is testing him and that a second character, the satan, has afflicted him. The reader's knowledge creates the pervasive irony of the book; the words of Job and his friends mean one thing to them and another to the reader. Job accuses God of being his enemy and entertains the hope there is another figure in heaven who will, as a neutral arbiter, mediate between them. The reader knows that God is not Job's enemy (God is interested in other matters) and that "the other figure," the cynical satan, is Job's enemy.

Job's explosion of anger in chapter 3 breaks the seven-day silence. His eloquent and intricate poetry ends the regular and stately prose of the prologue. "Curse God, and die!" advises his wife, but Job refuses. Job's curse is a catalytic action, according to H. Habel,[9] which creates a dramatic complication that is not resolved until his final words in 42:1-6. His curse, like his oath in 27:2-5 and challenge to God in 31:35-37, provokes a vigorous reaction from his friends. Much of their shock and anger arises not only from his speeches but from his opening curse and lament.

In its structure, Job's speech is a curse on the day he was born (vv. 3-10) and a lament, "Why?" (vv. 11-26). He wishes for pre-creation darkness and inertness. He complains that God has fenced him in with hostile intent (3:23), using the very words of the satan, who complained that God had fenced him about (1:10) to protect him. In the narrative plot, Job's reversal of creation, his refusal to accept it and to submit, will be the stuff of God's speech to him in chapters 38–42. Now, however, numbed by his grievous losses, he wishes he were dead, that is, in the darkness of Sheol.

THE FIRST CYCLE (CHAPTERS 3–14)

Chapter 3 is not only Job's declaration but also the first speech in the dialogue with his friends, Eliphaz of Teman, Bildad of Shua, and Zophar of Naamath. At times the speeches develop a well-known theme such as the retribution that always comes upon the unjust or the value of persistent prayer to God; at other times the speeches respond to a previous one. An example of one speech responding to another is 6:2-3, "O that my vexation *(ka'as)* were weighed, / and all my calamity laid in the balances! / For then it would be heavier than the sand of the sea," which responds to 5:2, "Surely vexation *(ka'as)* kills the fool." Some of the speeches repeat themes previously mentioned, but ancient arguments about divine justice and order (such as those in *A Man and His God* or *The Babylonian Theodicy*) did not compartmentalize their logic or their reasons. Each speech is from a sage, who, in true wisdom fashion, talks from his experience of the tradition.

Space constraints prevent detailed analysis of all the speeches. Despite patches of problematic text, the arguments are not difficult to follow even without a detailed commentary. I will examine the opening exchange of the first cycle, that between Eliphaz and Job (chaps. 4–7), and then make some comments about the *dramatic* progression of chapters 8–14. Eliphaz in chapters 4–5 has the longest speech of any of the friends. The content of his arguments is not novel (though the vision of 4:12-21 is remarkable by any standard): 4:1-6, a sage should be patient (not deliver himself of curses and laments as you, Job, just did in chapter 3); 4:7-11, don't worry, the universe has a way of turning on the wicked; 4:12-21, I had a personal dreamlike experience of just how transient and fragile human beings really are; 5:1-7, fools get alarmed, failing to realize that human beings are born for trouble; 5:8-16, seek God who can save you; 5:17-27, God is "disciplining" or teaching you by rough means but will bring you through this crisis. But content is not the whole of it. The speech is a transaction between two persons; its verbs are largely in the second person singular addressing Job; it invokes Eliphaz's personal experience as an authoritative source.

Job replies in chapters 6–7, his first speech.[10] Chapter 6 responds specifically to Eliphaz and chapter 7 makes a new argument. Chapter 6:2-7 responds to 5:2-7: to Eliphaz's statement that Job's troubles arise from his overheated mind ("vexation") and from human beings' tendency toward trouble, Job replies that his troubles arise rather from "the arrows of the Almighty"; God is the cause of his vexation. Chapter 6:8-13 responds to 4:2-6: Job's hope is not in his past revering of God and support of the needy but in his desire that God will end his existence. Job's real intent, however, is to criticize Eliphaz for failing to be a friend (6:14-27). The three look like friends but offer no support; they teach but they don't listen.

Job's frustration and anger at his friends echoes the emotional tone of *The Babylonian Theodicy* and other ancient complaints, which class loss of friends as a terrible affliction. Chapter 7 is an independent statement of the misery of human life. Each of its three sections (vv. 1-8, 9-16, 17-21) opens with an axiom on the human condition and ends with a taunt rather than with the plea that would be expected if these were normal laments. In its three panels, the poem depicts a "sufferer's cosmology," in Habel's phrase: *earth* is the place of oppressed human beings (v. 1), *Sheol* is where they will eventually arrive (vv. 9-10), and *heaven* is the home of their tormenter (vv. 17-18). Verses 17-21 are an exegetical revision of Psalm 8:4-7: "What are human beings that you are mindful of them, / mortals that you care for them? . . . You have given them dominion over the works of your hands; / you have put all things under their feet." Job takes over the psalm (identical Hebrew words italicized), *"What are human beings, that* you make so much of them, / that you set your mind on them, / visit them every morning, / test them every moment?"* (Job 7:17-18).[11] The divine attention that elicited awe and admiration from the psalmist elicits from Job anger and sarcasm: a hostile God is scrutinizing him. Job's world is collapsing. He seeks meaning and love and can find neither.

To conclude the first cycle (chaps. 8–14), I can but briefly note how the remaining speeches further the narrative plot and then comment on the important legal metaphor, introduced in 8:3, which begins to be developed in chapter 9.

Bildad frames the issue in legal language in 8:3, provoking Job to a new and spirited self-defense: "Does God pervert justice? Or does the Almighty pervert the right?" This form of the question will provoke Job's response in 9:2-4, "Of course I know that's true, / but how can a human being win a suit against God? / If one desire to go to court with him, / He would not answer one word in a thousand! / Totally wise, completely powerful, / who can oppose him and win?" (my translation).

Job's lengthy reply in chapters 9–10 does not fall into the neat units one finds in other speeches. Its coherence comes from the progression of its ideas. Provoked by Bildad's mention of the law, Job first declares legal recourse futile because of who God is (9:2-13), considers the odds nonetheless (9:14-24), explores some alternatives (9:25-35), imagines himself suing God (10:1-17), and only then declares it futile (10:18-22). Yet Job has entertained the possibility of suing God!

Zophar in chapter 11 responds with a sage's argument that does not seem, on first reading, to touch on Job's points. As Habel helpfully notes,[12] the friends reply to Job in three ways: (1) by citing an opponent's statement (as in 8:4); (2) by isolating a key motif and responding to that alone; (3) most frequently, by employing ironic innuendo, association, and wordplay. A close reading reveals that Zophar does all three in this chapter.

Chapters 12–14 contain Job's longest speech and the conclusion of the first cycle of speeches. Its second part (13:6-28) is legal, and its final part (chap. 14) sums up and concludes the argumentation of the first cycle. The second part builds on Job's earlier considera-tion of legal action, which he previously gave up as futile. In the meantime, the friends' ridiculing his claim of innocence has led him back to the idea. He will confront God, speak to his face ("face" is repeated several times), if only God will allow him to approach and speak unhindered. Job ends with a reflection on humans' lack of substance in the face of God's immensity, yet not completely abandoning a hope that "You would call, and I would answer you" (14:15). As the chapter ends, the reader knows the drama is not over. Job and his friends are alienated and so no help will arise from that quarter. God too is an enemy, yet Job is pondering a course of action.

Before proceeding to the unfolding drama in the second cycle, we must pause briefly to consider the legal metaphor in Job. Scholars in the last few decades have noticed the frequency of legal terminology in Job, for example, in the verbs to declare guilty, to declare innocent, to go to court. The terms also have a nonjuridical meaning, for the three legal idioms in the foregoing sentence can also mean simply to act wickedly, to act without guilt, to argue. The legal nuance can easily be missed. In the ancient world, law was important and a common source of metaphors for describing the relation between the gods and the human world. Job is looked upon by his friends as "guilty," for why else would he be suffering his terrible ordeal? To combat his friends and to confront God, Job must use legal language.

One aspect of the legal metaphor drives the plot forward. Job hopes for an umpire (*môkîah*, 9:33), though he acknowledges that such a figure probably does not exist. In 16:18-22, he hopes that his blood will cry out against the injustice done to him and a heavenly witness will appear to arbitrate his case. The mediator someday will appear in court to vindicate him, "For I know that my Redeemer lives, / and that at the last he will stand upon the earth." In his great testimony in chapters 29–31, Job testifies to his innocence even though no court has been convened. He takes a formal oath of innocence in chapter 31 and expresses the heartfelt wish that he had someone to hear him, that his adversary at law would appear (31:35). The best dramatic explanation for the sudden and unexpected appearance of Elihu in chapters 32–37 is that Elihu is stepping forward as just that mediator. When Yahweh appears to Job, he characterizes Job in 40:1 as "the one with a suit against the Almighty, . . . the one arraigning Eloah" (Habel's translation). Yahweh's mighty questions against Job are those of the courtroom. In the end, Job withdraws his case ("Therefore I retract and repent of dust and ashes"), his retraction ending the conflict between himself and God. One point of the book is to show that to judge God on the basis of human justice is futile.

THE SECOND CYCLE (CHAPTERS 15–21)

By this time, the reader should know how to read the speeches; any one of several topics can be developed, and a topic is often stated first as an axiom. The responses by Job or by his friends are not point for point but indirect (citation, wordplay, allusion). In the second cycle, relations between Job and his friends grow worse, inevitably focusing attention on the one relationship left to Job, his relationship to God. The speeches are shorter in the second cycle, but Job's responses are more trenchant.

Eliphaz, who responded first to Job in chapters 4–5, begins the new series in chapter 15, but this time as a savage critic rather than a sympathetic friend. Job, he says, you are attacking piety itself (v. 4) and speaking as if you were the first man who enjoyed the knowledge of the gods. Then he restates again his belief that the wicked are punished.

In chapters 16–17 Job states bluntly that God attacked him, "I was prospering, and he broke me in two" (16:12), and "he rushes at me like a warrior" (16:14). Where can he turn? Not to his friends, for "there are mockers around me" (17:2). His only hope is the witness in heaven, first broached in 9:33 and rejected as impossible (16:18-19, 21): "O earth, do not cover my blood; / let my outcry find no resting place. / Even now, in fact, my witness is in heaven, / and he that vouches for me is on high. . . . that he would maintain the right of a mortal with God, / as one does for a neighbor." Who is this arbiter?

Certainly not God, despite a few commentators who claim a merciful and just God will overthrow the cruel God attacking Job, for the mediator will be *between* God and Job. Job evidently calls for an (unspecified) member of the heavenly court, but the reader, who knows far more than Job, is aware that the only court member active up to this point is the satan. And the satan will win a wager only if Job does *not* persevere in his integrity! In response to Job's pathetic hope, Bildad vehemently restates the iron law of retribution on the wicked.

Job 19 is one of the justly famous passages in the Bible, and verses 25-27 ("I know that my Redeemer lives") was set to immortal music by G. F. Handel in *Messiah*.

> Have pity on me, have pity on me, O you my friends,
>   for the hand of God has touched me!
> Why do you, like God, pursue me,
>   never satisfied with my flesh?
> "O that my words were written down!
>   O that they were inscribed in a book!
> O that with an iron pen and with lead
>   they were engraved on a rock forever!
> For I know that my Redeemer lives,
>   and that at the last he will stand upon the earth;
> and after my skin has been thus destroyed,
>   then in my flesh I shall see God,
> whom I shall see on my side,
>   and my eyes shall behold, and not another.
> My heart faints within me!
> If you say, 'How we will persecute him!'
>   and, 'The root of the matter is found in him';
> be afraid of the sword,
>   for wrath brings the punishment of the sword,
>   so that you may know there is a judgment."

Unfortunately the Hebrew text is uncertain. The two dominant interpretations of the redeemer are that it is either God or a figure in the heavenly court. The latter makes by far the best sense in the narrative. His friends do not support him ("pity me" is ironic). Job is sure he will die, for God is his enemy. His one hope is that after his death someone in the heavens will stand up for him and declare him innocent. Job is unyielding: he is innocent of the kind of wrongdoing that would bring such horrific suffering, and will maintain his innocence to his death. Job's desire to be proved blameless after his death runs into Zophar's appeal to ancient tradition (cf. chap. 8) that the exulting of the wicked is only momentary (8:5). Job's final speech of the second cycle (chapter 21) summarizes much of the early material.

THE THIRD CYCLE (CHAPTERS 22–27)

The third cycle is even shorter than the second, suggesting that the author assumes the reader has heard the basic arguments and most of their variations. Dramatically, the third cycle enlarges on the incompatibility of the two sets of ideas about suffering and divine justice, further illustrates the gap between Job and his friends, and makes very clear that Job is completely isolated. In chapter 27 Job concludes his conversation with his comforters.

The third cycle has unfortunately suffered textual damage with the result that some sections can no longer be attributed to their proper speaker. The following passages are widely recognized to be out of place in their present position in the Hebrew text: 24:18-24 occurs in a speech of Job but the sentiments are wholly those of the friends; 26:1-4, which belongs to Job, falls within a speech of Bildad (25:1-6 plus 26:5-14); 27:13-24 occurs in a speech of Job but is only appropriate to one of the friends. Full discussion of the problem along with suggested attributions can be found in any large commentary. I assume with the majority of scholars that 24:18-24 belongs to one of the friends, probably Zophar (though it may not be complete), that Job's speech in 26:1-4 prefaces his speech in 27:2-12, and that 27:13-23 belongs to Zophar, continuing themes of his previous speech in chapter 20. It should be noted, however, that some scholars accept the text as is, proposing that in 24:18-24 Job speaks in a concessive vein, that in 26:5-14 Job contemptuously finishes Bildad's speech for him, and that 27:13-23 is a parody of what he might expect to hear from Zophar.[13] Such interpretations are ingenious, but the author of Job gives no hint to the reader of these subtle shifts.

Eliphaz's third and final speech (chap. 22) is a far cry from his opening speech (chaps. 4–5), which was conciliatory and sympathetic to Job who had just cursed the day of his birth in chapter 3. Eliphaz accuses Job of a series of typical crimes (vv. 6-9), which explains why Job is suffering so severely. Yet, says Eliphaz, there is still time for repentance. Job's response in chapter 23 is to press his lawsuit, expressing the ardent wish to come to God's dwelling to rehearse it in God's very face. Job has expressed hopes before, using the Hebrew idiom "Oh that I might . . ." *(mî yittēn)*. In 6:8-9, he hoped that God would stamp him out; in 14:13, that God would hide him in Sheol until the divine anger was spent; in 19:22, that his case would be recorded for his redeemer to use after Job's death. Here, he hopes that he can find God's abode so he can present his case directly. In the final instance of the phrase (31:35-37), Job hopes that God would appear and give Job a hearing. The successive occurrences of the phrase make Job's goals clear. At the beginning, when he was still stunned, he wanted surcease. After debating with his friends, he wants confrontation with God even though, as he admits in verses 15-17, the prospect terrifies him. In the closely connected chapter 24, Job explains why he fears coming near God: "Even those close to him cannot foresee his actions" *(Tanakh)*. He next lists, in a poignant passage, the needy people to whom God pays not the slightest attention (24:5-17; we adopt Habel's rendering of v. 5a, "Others are like wild asses").

Bildad in 25:1-6 plus 26:5-14 points to the massive universe under the exquisite control of the creator as proof that no human being can be righteous before God. How can Job demand anything of such a God? Job's final speech is in slight disorder. It begins in 26:1-4 and continues immediately in 27:1 forward. Modern readers quickly sense that 27:1-12, which begins with a powerful oath, must mark a turn: "As God lives, who has taken away my right, / and the Almighty, who has made my soul bitter, / as long as my breath is in me / and the spirit of God is in my nostrils, / my lips will not speak falsehood, / and my tongue will not utter deceit" (27:2-4). The oath invokes God as the guarantor, who will ensure that a broken oath will be punished. Job refuses to say his friends are right and holds on to his innocence (vv. 5-6). In 27:7, Job speaks of his enemy (singular), which seems to be a reference to God. The context is legal. Job wishes to be declared innocent and his "enemy" to be declared guilty. If God were the victor and Job the guilty party (NRSV "unrighteous"), his life as an outcast would be intolerable (27:9-10). Job has experienced "the hand" (= power) of God sufficiently (27:11-12). Job's speech, brief as it is, shows his impossible situation: his oath invokes God as a guarantor of his truthfulness, but the same God has prejudged him. Another indication of a turning point is that 27:1-12 reprises the prologue (chaps. 1–2): God is the one who took away Job's right (see 1:12; 2:6), affirming he has not spoken falsehood (see 1:22; 2:10) nor put away his integrity (see 1:8). What will happen next?

THE POEM ON WISDOM (CHAPTER 28)

Something new takes place in the story—an independent, lengthy poem on wisdom. Because it is spoken by the narrator rather than by Job or the friends, chapter 28 stands alone. All commentators admire its structure and logic, but assess its place in the book of Job in quite different ways. Many believe it is a later insertion, a pious addition to soften Job's demands to face God and get to the truth of his case. If one assumes that Job is a story, however, delaying or "retarding" the action at a key moment by an unexpected speech makes good dramatic sense. In the absence of textual evidence to the contrary, one should assume the speech is original to the book. In fact, the chapter accomplishes several things. Dramatically, retarding the action raises questions and expectations in the reader's mind. What will happen to Job's impossible oath? It also transposes a central question of the dialogues—how can human beings presume to know God's ways?—to a plane that is nondialectic and hymnic.

What does the poem say? Structurally and thematically, the hymn celebrates the *inaccessibility* of wisdom. Human beings, who are able to search out the hiding places of precious stones (vv. 1-6, 9-11, 13), animals, who view areas never seen by the human race (vv. 7-8, 21), the great ocean (v. 14), and Sheol (v. 22), do not know the way to wisdom. Only God knows (v. 23) and the only way to it is "fear of the Lord . . . to depart from evil" (v. 28). In structure, there are three sections, verses 1-11, 12-19, and 20-28. Key words are "place" *(māqôm)*, "way" *(derek)*, "to search" *(ḥāqar)*, and "to see" *(rā 'â)*.[14]

How does the poem *function* in the book of Job? First, by declaring that no human being knows the way to wisdom, it suggests what the reader already knows, that the dialogue between the friends and Job cannot provide a satisfactory conclusion to the problem of Job. If there is to be an answer, the hymn suggests, it will come from "another quarter" (Esth 4:14), thus pointing the way to the theophany of chapters 38-41. The poem also interprets wisdom as *cosmic* wisdom: "When he gave to the wind its weight, / and apportioned out the waters by measure; / when he made a decree for the rain, / and a way for the thunderbolt" (vv. 25-26). The cosmic perspective is a shift from the historical and personal viewpoint of Job and points forward to the cosmic perspective in the divine speeches.

THE FINAL SPEECH OF JOB (CHAPTERS 29–31)

Chapters 29–31 are Job's final statement, not a dialogue but a great monologue, and the longest speech of the book until the divine speeches in chapters 38–41. In 27:1-2 he took an oath to tell the truth, invoking God to punish him if he lied. These chapters are his testimony before the court and a legal challenge to God. In chapter 29 Job portrays himself as an ideal ruler, perfectly fulfilling his role as chief in the community. He uses language of himself that could also be used of God, for example, "the light of my countenance" (v. 24), which evokes "the light of [God's] face" in Psalms 4:7; 44:4; 89:16; cf. Numbers 6:25. Job's description of himself is, to say the least, provocative.

But now, says Job in his complaint (chap. 30), he has been humiliated and attacked. He is attacked by the basest elements of society (vv. 1-14) and by the terrors of God (vv. 15-19). Verses 20-31 turn to God ("you") with the accusation that God has denied Job the justice that Job practiced toward others as a ruler. The verb "to cry out" (vv. 20, 24, 28) unifies the accusation: Job cries out to God and gets no answer; Job answered the poor when they cried out to him; when Job cries out in the assembly no one answers. Job's reiteration of "cry out [for justice]" raises the stakes. Can the God of justice remain silent?

In chapter 31 (continuing 27:2-4) Job swears an oath to clear himself of all the charges against him: "If I ever did such and such, may such and such happen to me!" The negative confession has a chiastic structure.[15]

A   Covenant and its curse (vv. 1-3)
   B   Challenge: weigh me in a balance of justice (God has *counted* [Hebrew root *spr*] Job's *steps*) (vv. 4-6)
      C   [catalog of crimes] (vv. 7-34)
   B′   Challenge: provide a legal document *(sēper)*; then Job will repeat the *count (spr)* of his *steps* before God (vv. 35-37)
A′   Covenant witness and curse (vv. 38-40) (earth is sometimes invoked as covenant witness)

Job makes a declaration of his own virtue, portraying himself to the court as a hero without parallel in his motivation or performance. In fact, he is not claiming for himself more than God had said of him in 1:8 and 2:3. Job's catalog, however, is provocative, for it implies that God is an irrational destroyer of people of integrity.

The speech ends with a legal demand: "Oh, if only I had someone to conduct a hearing for me! / Here is my signature, let the Almighty prepare a response! / Let my adversary at law draft a document" (31:35 my translation). Job's wish for legal redress has come full circle. He initiated a suit (10:2), declared himself ready to follow it (13:13-18), and several times expressed the hope for a legal mediator (9:33; 16:19; 19:25).

ELIHU'S SPEECHES (CHAPTERS 32–37)

The four Elihu speeches (chaps. 32–33; 34, 35, and 36) are judged by many commentators to be secondary, an attempt by a later writer to respond to Job's arguments more effectively than the friends did. One indication of its secondary nature is 42:7, which speaks of "you [Eliphaz] and your *two* friends," and 42:9, which mentions only the three friends of the dialogues. It is often interpreted to suggest Elihu is not original. The arguments for the originality of Elihu's speeches are more persuasive, however: (1) Elihu is a comic figure, a youth claiming to be wiser than his elders, a wise man dominated by anger (the mark of a fool, 32:2-5), whose belly is like unvented wine, ready to explode (32:19); (2) Job had expressed the hope for a mediator between himself (9:33; 16:19; 19:25) and the hope that Yahweh would appear, but Elihu is the farcical answer to his prayers; (3) the omission of Elihu from the epilogue simply acknowledges that only the three friends and Job are the real actors in the drama; Elihu is an interloper; (4) Elihu's appearance prepares for Yahweh's later appearance, and his topics, in particular divine justice, design, and cosmic wisdom prepare the reader for those same topics in the Yahweh speeches. If a later author intended to respond to Job's arguments by means of Elihu's speeches, would the later author make Elihu a figure of fun? True, the "retarding" action of Elihu seems excessive to a modern reader, but the ancients loved rhetorical fullness.

Elihu's arguments are not difficult to grasp. His speeches will appear blustery and meandering unless one has some sense of their design. Chapter 32 introduces Elihu, illustrating the contradiction that exists between Elihu's content (his claim to be a sage) and his style (the self-importance and volubility of a fool). Chapter 33 specifically addresses Job's complaint that God did not respond to him. Elihu says that God speaks to people in many different ways (the key word "the Pit" recurs three times)—through dreams (vv. 15-18), through suffering (vv. 19-22), and through healing (vv. 23-28). Unlike the three friends, Elihu quotes Job; for example 33:1-11 plus 31-33 cites Job's speech in 13:17-28. Elihu's second speech (chap. 34) cites Job's sentiments (27:2-6) in verses 5-6 to belittle his character (vv. 7-9). Elihu defends God's character in verses 10-15 (God never does wrong!), defends God's governance as just (God condemns the wicked and upholds the righteous poor) and as not subject to human scrutiny in verses 16-30, and finally urges Job to repent. Chapter 35 attacks Job for his sense of entitlement (vv. 2-4). How can Job expect reward from God, for God is too far removed from Job to be affected by his conduct (vv. 5-8)? Besides, given that most cries for help are insincere it is no wonder that God does not hearken to them (vv. 9-13). Job has no right to complain (vv. 14-16).

The fourth and final speech of Elihu consists of three parts. Each part begins with an address to Job (36:2-4; 36:16-21; 37:14-22) and moves on to portray God as just and wise (36:5-15; 36:22-25; 37:23-24). Elihu focuses on the storm as the great symbol of divine power and wisdom (36:26-37:13). In 36:5-15, Elihu points out that God, "mighty in strength of understanding" (36:5) in justice "does not keep the wicked alive" (36:6) and in wisdom educates by disciplining those who stray (36:7-15). The storm is a divine masterpiece, a vivid illustration of divine wisdom and power (36:26-37:13). Elihu ends with a series of taunting questions to Job, unwittingly foreshadowing the coming speech of Yahweh, for example, "Can you, like him, spread out the skies?" (37:18). But it is in his final statement that the irony of Elihu comes to full and climactic expression: "The Almighty—we cannot find him; / he is great in power and justice, / and abundant righteousness he will not violate. / Therefore mortals fear him; / he does not regard any who are wise in their own conceit."[16]

YAHWEH'S SPEECHES (CHAPTERS 38–42)

The opening line of chapter 38, "Then the LORD answered Job out of the whirlwind," has been prepared for by Job's demand to see God and by his heroic speech and oath in chapters 27 plus 29-31 and, in an ironic way, by Elihu's "epiphany" and final statement. Yet the sentence never fails to surprise. What mere mortal can summon God, or, if God appears, remain alive long enough for conversation? The reader of the book has, nonetheless, waited long for something dramatic to happen, hearing out the friends until their arguments have become almost too familiar, bearing with Job even as he

isolates himself, listening to the bombast of Elihu. Thus the
theophany, no matter how irregular in the religion of the time, has
a certain logic in the book. God has been, after all, the silent actor,
constantly spoken *about* by the friends, constantly spoken *to* by Job.

God responds to Job in two lengthy speeches (chaps. 38–39 and
40–41), each ending with a short response by Job (40:1-5 and 42:1-6).
But how do the speeches respond to Job's complaint? The logic of the
two speeches has puzzled many scholars and provoked many rear-
rangements; no rearrangement has won general assent. A significant
minority of scholars regard the speeches to be without logic; they are
thunderous explosions meant to humble or threaten Job, and
communicate the message that there is no rational answer to
Job's question. Such scholars rightly perceive that Yahweh's
response is not a matter of reasonable arguments but the
thunder of a God who is not on the same ontological level as
Job. As Job's discussions with the three friends were not only a
matter of logic but involved emotions and human relationships
and community, so also God's speeches belong to the commu-
nication and relationship of creator to creature. Still, the
speeches are carefully wrought, with a logic and a design of
their own. One of the most persuasive literary analyses is Habel's, who accepts the Hebrew text as it stands.[17]

God responds to two charges: governing the world unwisely
and unjustly. God handles the first complaint—unwise or capricious governance—in his first speech (38:1–40:5), beginning,
"Who is this who obscures *design ('ēṣâ)?*"[18] The second complaint is against unjust governance. It should be noted that
justice is to be taken in a biblical sense: the inability or failure to
uphold the rights of the aggrieved innocent. This charge is
answered in the second speech (40:6–41:26), beginning, "Will
you impugn my *justice?*"

The two speeches form large-scale parallelism, which would have
produced resonances for ancient hearers. The force of the speeches
is better shown by Habel's outline than by extensive quotation.[19]

A Introductory	38:1	*A1* Introductory	40:6
formula with report		formula with report of	
of theophany event		theophany event	
B Thematic challenge	38:2-3	*B1* Thematic challenge	40:7-14
i Theme A		*i* Theme B	
"Who is this		"Would you	

89

who clouds my *design?"*	impugn my *justice?"*
ii Summons "Gird your loins"	ii Summons "Gird your loins"
C Elaboration of theme	C1 *Elaboration of theme*
i in the physical 38:4-38 world	i with Behemoth 40:15-24
ii in the animal 38:39 kingdom	ii with Leviathan 40:25-41:26
D Challenge to Legal Adversary 40:1-2	
E Answer of Job 40:3-5	E1 Answer of Job 42:1-6

A. The first speech. Job has denied God's wisdom by emphasizing God's unwise or arbitrary positioning of the elements of the world—mountains, seas, and so forth—and his failure to care for his creatures, especially Job. God responds in the legal idiom of Job's attack. The divine questions are legal in nature: "Who is this who obscures design?" (38:2); and later, "Where were you when I . . . ?" "Who placed . . . ?" "Where is . . . ?" They equivalently ask who created the world, and resemble questions in the great trial scenes of Second Isaiah such as, "Who has measured the waters in the hollow of his hand?" (40:12); "Who has directed the spirit of Yahweh?" (40:13); "Who has stirred up one from the east?" (41:2); "Who declared it from the beginning that we might know?" (44:7). In the book of Job the questions have the same intent: to remind Job that God, not Job, is God. Only a deity could answer them affirmatively. It was Job who set the legal context in chapters 29–31, when he hailed God into court.

As in the speeches of Job and Bildad, the depiction of the universe is traditional: God's artisanlike building of the universe, hemming in of sea, and placement of heavenly luminaries. What is untraditional is the challenge these elements pose to Job. Throughout the book Job has been seeking a face-to-face encounter with God. In the encounter itself, God treats Job as a rival claimant to deity, asking him questions only a deity would be able to answer affirmatively. Can Job play God, bring a universe into being, sustain it, and control it?

A general outline illustrates this last point more clearly than any single verse. The first divine speech, chapters 38–39, can be schematized as follows:

Were you there? or, do you know about
A. the inanimate physical world (38:4-38)?
   —the construction of the earth 38:4-7
   —the hemming in of the sea 38:8-11
   —dawn's role in ridding the earth of sinners 38:12-15
   —God's dominion over the underworld of death 38:16-18
   —the placement of light and darkness 38:19-21
   —the storehouses of earth's weather 38:22-30
   —the constellations controlling earth's destiny 38:31-33
   —the thunderstorms fertilizing the earth 38:34-38, and
B. the animal and bird kingdoms (38:39–39:30)?
   —the feeding of the lion 38:39-40
   —the feeding of the raven 38:41
   —the ibex and the hind 39:1-4
   —the wild ass 39:5-8
   —the wild ox 39:9-12
   —the ostrich 39:13-18
   —the horse 39:19-25
   —the hawk and the eagle 39:26-30.

The speech is about "design" or wisdom (38:2). Job had accused God in 9:5-6 of making a reckless and violent attack upon mountains and earth: "he who removes mountains, and they do not know it, / when he overturns them in his anger; / who shakes the earth out of its place, / and its pillars tremble." God asks Job in 38:4-7 if he actually witnessed the foundation of the earth, and then reveals how, like a careful artisan, he built with measuring line, sockets, and cornerstone while a festive chorus sang as at a temple dedication. In 9:24 Job had claimed that God does not distinguish between the wicked and the righteous, that the earth has been handed over to the wicked. God responds that dawn exposes the deeds done by the wicked during the night, but that he does not necessarily punish them (38:12-15). Job's assumption that human beings are the center of the world is countered by God's question about the rain that falls where human beings do not live (38:26-27). Job had accused God of hunting him like a lion (10:16); God is rather the one who hunts *for* the lion (38:39-40). Even the ostrich, proverbial for its stupidity, is so by design (39:13-18), a reminder that God's design does not operate exclusively for human beings or rational purposes. It includes the useful, the bizarre, even the playful. God creates for his inscrutable purposes; even Behemoth and Leviathan are admirable in the divine sight. God creates for God, not for human beings, and need not answer the single-minded Job who assumes he is the center of the universe.

Just before Job's response to this catalog, God again affirms the legal context: "Will the one with a suit against Shadday correct me? Will the one arraigning Eloah answer me?" (40:2 Habel's translation).[20] Job's answer is also legal: "See, I am of small account; what shall I answer you? / I lay my hand on my mouth. / I have spoken once, and I will not answer; / twice, but will proceed no further" (40:4-5). The words are a promise not to speak, an acknowledgment that he is dropping his suit (not that he repents in a religious sense).

B. The second speech. The second speech, 40:6–41:26, is a defense of God's justice impugned by Job. I translate 40:8, "Would you impugn my justice?" Justice here, as commonly in the Bible, does not consist in neutral objectivity that renders a just verdict but consists in partisan intervention on behalf of the aggrieved party. It is exercised in activity, putting down the unjust and upholding the just. From Job's perspective, God has allowed the wicked to prosper and the righteous, in particular Job, to suffer. God initially asks questions that only a deity could answer affirmatively: "Have you an arm like God, / and can you thunder with a voice like his? . . . Look on all who are proud, and bring them low; / tread down the wicked where they stand" (40:9, 12). Job falls silent because he cannot be just in this cosmic sense.

God's speech is surprising. It is almost wholly devoted to describing two great animals: Behemoth (40:15-24) and Leviathan (40:25–41:26). Behemoth has been identified by many modern commentators as the hippopotamus, that is, simply a powerful and frightening animal, but this is unlikely. His mate, Leviathan, is obviously a mythological beast, which is clear from the Ugaritic texts that show him allied with Sea, the storm god Baal's enemy. The Bible has the same usage. In *1 Enoch* 60:7-9, Leviathan and Behemoth are creatures, respectively, of the depths of the sea and of the immense desert.[21] Behemoth is thus a creature symbolizing the sterile wilderness (in the Ugaritic texts, the milieu of the god Mot, Baal's enemy).

The first speech answered the charge of unwise governance by demonstrating God's care for an intricate world that Job scarcely knows. The second speech answers Job's charge of unjust governance by showing that God has power over cosmic evil, represented by Behemoth and Leviathan. God does not say that he always controls evil for the sake of human beings, but that he can if he wants. The question put to Job is—can you contain these animals and so prove you are God?

The two beasts are proposed as examples of exulting power. The massive Behemoth (40:15-26) is made as Job was (v. 15); that is, he is a creature like him. For all Behemoth's strength, however, he can be taken by the face: "By his eyes he is captured, / by hooks his nose is pierced" (40:24).[22]

The second portrait, Leviathan, is much longer than the first. Leviathan is known from the Bible and from the Ugaritic texts as the great primordial monster who was killed or tamed by Baal or Yahweh. As with Behemoth, God controls him by the mouth (41:1-2).

> [10]There is no one so fierce as to stir him up.
>   Who then can stand before *me?*
> [11]Whoever challenges me I will requite,
>   For everything under heaven is mine.
> [12]Did I not silence his boasting,
>   his mighty words and martial deeds? (my translation)

Magnificent and laudatory poetry follows, describing Leviathan as built for no other purpose than to display untrammeled power and might.

What is the purpose of these two beasts in the book? In 40:12, God defined justice (which Job claimed is lacking in the universe) by the command, "Look down upon every proud one and bring him low, and tread upon the wicked where they stand." The two beasts exemplify fearsome power that is beyond human knowledge or control, yet they are allowed a place in God's universe. They fulfill no function; they cannot be domesticated and do not serve human beings. Though they are under divine control (40:15, 24; 41:2-4), God, for reasons not stated, allows them to exist despite their evil potential. Jon Levenson, properly taking issue with the common view that Behemoth and Leviathan are mere playthings in God's hand, notes that "whereas Job 40–41 explicitly states that Behemoth is a work of God, no such statement is made of Leviathan in the much longer section devoted to him. Instead, we hear only of God's heroic capture and conquest of the great sea beast."[23] In the literary structure of the book, the beasts echo the satan of chapters 1 and 2, whom God allowed to "incite" him (2:3). Why should there be an enemy of the human race within the heavenly court itself? No answer is given to this particular problem of evil, beyond the assurance that the Adversary, like the beasts, is somehow under the control of God. God retains control over the beasts as over the Adversary: "All that [Job] has is in your power; only do not stretch out your hand against him!" (1:12); "Very well, he is in your power; only spare his life" (2:6). There is no guarantee, however, that evil will not ravage human beings.

The universe in the book of Job has been created by a God, utterly transcendent in wisdom and justice. The universe cannot be analyzed by human beings (chap. 28) and summed up with traditional wisdom, as is shown by the three friends' inability to speak the truth about God (42:7-8). God creates for God; the divine purpose is inscrutable; human beings cannot assume that they are the center of the universe. Traditional creation accounts in the ancient Near East often began with the gods vanquishing evil, which was often personified as a monster. But creation in the book of Job *ends* with the monsters unvanquished, with God admiring them in splendid poetry! They are, to be sure, on God's leash, but they move in ways that threaten and terrify the human race.

Job's preoccupation with his own case led him to narrow his focus and concentrate on the human race and on himself. This anthropocentric perspective is rebutted by God. Moshe Greenberg reflects on the Joban perspective:

How different this survey of creation [chaps. 38–41] is from that of Genesis 1 or the hymn to nature of Psalm 104. Here man is incidental—mainly an impotent foil to God. In Genesis 1 (and its echo, Ps. 8) teleology pervades a process of creation whose goal and crown is man. All is directed to his benefit; the earth and its creatures are his to rule. In Psalm 104 nature exhibits a providential harmony of which man is an integral part. But the God of Job celebrates each act and product of his creation for itself, an independent value attesting his power and grace. Job, representing mankind, stands outside the picture, displaced from its center to a remote periphery.[24]

Job responds to the second speech in one of the most eloquent passages in the Bible (42:2-6 my translation):

I know you can do everything,
    nothing you propose is beyond you.
[You said:] "Who is this that obscures my design without knowledge?"

Indeed, I spoke without understanding,
of things beyond me, which I did not know.
[You said:] "Hear now and I will speak,
I will do the questioning and you will respond."
I have heard of you by the hearing of the ears,
but now my eye sees you.
Therefore I retract
and give up my dust and ashes.

The bracketed words are supplied in the assumption that Job is citing God (just as God had cited Job). Verse 6 here differs from its traditional translation, as in the NRSV, "Therefore I despise myself, / and repent in dust and ashes." The Hebrew verb in verse 6b with the preposition means "to change one's mind about." Job has decided to withdraw his lawsuit against God and to put off his "dust and ashes," the traditional costume of a lamenter and complainant. Why? Because his "eye" now sees God, which was his goal from the time he began to fight against his friends.

THE EPILOGUE (42:7-17)

The prose brings the reader back to the prologue (chaps. 1–2). We learn that God is angry against the three friends, for they "have not spoken the truth about me as my servant Job has" (v. 7). Job intercedes for them as he did for his own children in chapter 1 and his intercession wins forgiveness for them. The rest is quickly told. The Lord gives Job twice as much as he had before. His large family comes to console him, his domestic animals and his children are restored. He goes on to live one hundred and forty years and dies in peace.

How is one to interpret this epilogue? Those who begin their reading of Job with the *problem* of reconciling the prose and the poetry, Job the patient and Job the impatient, may regard the prologue and epilogue as the original story. Those who begin with the assumption of unity will probably seek in the beginning and end the key to the work.

What does the epilogue (and the prologue) tell us about Job? First, it tells us that Job's protests and even accusations against God were, strange as it may seem, "telling the truth" about God (see 42:7). Job has withdrawn his suit, but Yahweh speaks admiringly of him, just as he did in 1:8 and 2:3, and blesses him above others.[25] Second, the prologue and epilogue imply (like the divine speeches) that the universe is entirely God's; it is theocentric, not anthropocentric. Job's travails arose because of a wager in the divine assembly between God and the satan, about which Job knew nothing. God essentially says the same to Job in the divine speeches. Yet Yahweh remains Job's God, who, in God's own way, is respectful of Job.

RECOMMENDED READING

Commentaries

Dhorme, Édouard. *A Commentary on the Book of Job*. Trans. H. Knight. New York: Nelson, 1967 (French original 1926). Excellent introductory essays especially on the theological meaning.

Habel, Norman. *The Book of Job*. Old Testament Library. Philadelphia: Westminster, 1985. A literary reading of Job, which does not neglect the language problems of the book. The most satisfactory large commentary.

Janzen, J. Gerald. *Job*. Interpretation; Atlanta: John Knox, 1985. A theological reading, original and provocative.

Pope, Marvin. *Job*. 3rd ed. Anchor Bible 15. Garden City, N.Y.: Doubleday, 1973. Lively translation; it incorporates many new linguistic suggestions.

Collections of Interpretive Essays

Glatzer, Nahum, ed. *The Dimensions of Job*. New York: Schocken, 1969.

Perdue, Leo, and W. Clark Gilpin, eds. *The Voice from the Whirlwind: Interpreting the Book of Job*. Nashville: Abingdon Press, 1992.

Sanders, Paul, ed. *Twentieth Century Interpretations of the Book of Job*. Englewood Cliffs, N.J.: Prentice-Hall, 1968.

Zuck, R. B., ed. *Sitting with Job: Selected Studies on the Book of Job*. Grand Rapids, Mich.: Baker, 1992.

CHAPTER 5

THE BOOK
OF QOHELETH
(ECCLESIASTES)

The author uses the name Qoheleth, "The Words of Qoheleth, son of David, King in Jerusalem." Grammatically, Qoheleth is the participle of the Hebrew verb *qāhal*, "to assemble, to gather." The feminine participle here seems to designate a functionary, someone who performs a recognized task. Qoheleth designates someone who gathers or collects wisdom writings. Ecclesiastes is the Latinized form of the Greek translation of the Hebrew word. The book is also sometimes called "The Preacher."

Our approach to Qoheleth will be like that for Job and Wisdom of Solomon; that is, the reader will be guided through the entire book. Qoheleth (and Job and Wisdom of Solomon) is not an anthology like Proverbs and Sirach, but demands to be read through as a coherent work.

GENRE

To modern sensibilities, the book may seem shockingly pessimistic and even nihilistic. It reminds us that ancient wisdom litera-

97

ture had a bleak and cynical strain. In Egyptian literature *The Dispute Between a Man and His Ba* (*AEL*, vol. 1, pp. 163-69) catalogs the difficulties of life, considers several options including suicide, and finally decides that living is still better than death: "Follow the feast day, forget worry!" "Harpers' Songs" (*AEL*, vol. 1, pp. 193-97; vol. 2, pp. 115-16) are tomb inscriptions that speak of the inevitability of death but then urge enjoyment of life. *The Complaints of Khakheperre-Sonb* (*AEL*, vol. 1, pp. 145-49) is a meditation on the misery that arises from civic instability and human treachery. Other works are similar in tone and topic, for example, *The Prophecies of Neferti* (*AEL*, vol. 1, pp. 139-45) and *The Admonitions of Ipuwer* (*AEL*, vol. 1, pp. 149-63).

The *e-dubba* or "tablet house" in Mesopotamia produced similar literature, including sharply satirical works. A good example from Mesopotamia is the eighteenth-century epic *Atrahasis* (*MFM*, 1-38; *BM*, vol. 1, pp. 158-201), which portrays the high god Enlil as a bumbling coward and the assembly of the gods as shortsighted and impetuous about the human race. *The Babylonian Theodicy* (*BWL*, 63-91 = *BM*, vol. 2, pp. 806-14), *The Counsels of a Pessimist* (*BWL*, 107-9), and *The Dialogue of Pessimism* (*BWL*, 139-49; *BM*, vol. 1, pp. 815-19) highlight the misery and uncertainty of human life. These works show that the skeptical and bleak tone of Qoheleth is not unique in the ancient world.

With one Mesopotamian classic Qoheleth has a special affinity—*Gilgamesh* in its standard version.[1] Both share a common theme—mortality—and speak of life under the sun, the days that have been determined for human existence, and the "vanity" of human achievement. "Wind" in *Gilgamesh* functions similarly to *hebel*, "breath," in Qoheleth. The ancient proverb of Qoheleth 4:12, "a three-ply cord is not easily broken," occurs also in *Gilgamesh*. Qoheleth 9:7-9 (with the identical sequence of topics) is found in the mouth of Siduri, the ale-wife or tavern-keeper in *Gilgamesh* (Old Babylonian version).

> Gilgamesh, whither rovest thou?
> The life thou pursuest thou shalt not find.
> When the gods created mankind,
> Death for mankind they set aside,
> Life in their own hands retaining.
> Thou, Gilgamesh, let full be thy belly,
> Make thou merry by day and by night.

Of each day make thou a feast of rejoicing,
Day and night dance thou and play!
Let thy garments be sparkling fresh,
Thy head be washed; bathe thou in water.
Pay heed to the little one that holds on to thy hand.
Let thy spouse delight in thy bosom!
For this is the task [of mankind!]]²

The most important contribution of *Gilgamesh* to Qoheleth, how-ever, is the light the standard version sheds on the genre of Qoheleth. The standard version of *Gilgamesh* added to the Old Babylonian version a prologue and an epilogue, which transformed a story of heroic exploits into an "autobiographical" narrative of a king. The prologue sings of the king in his old age, "[of him who] experienced everything, [I shall tea]ch the whole. . . . He who ex-perienced the whole gained complete wisdom. . . . He had jour-neyed far and wide, weary and at last resigned. He engraved all toils on a memorial monument of stone." The reader is then addressed in the second person: "Look for the copper tablet-box, / Undo its bronze lock, / Open the door to its secret, / Lift out the lapis lazuli tablet and read it, / The story of that man, Gilgamesh, who went through all kinds of sufferings."[3] Gilgamesh the warrior has be-come Gilgamesh the sage. Similarly, in Qoheleth 1–2 the great king tells us of his vast experience that is the basis of his wisdom. Having established his *persona* in chapters 1–2 as the legendary king who has seen and done everything, Qoheleth uses "I" to the very end of the book. In no other biblical wisdom book does an author explicitly base all his teaching on his *personal* experience and observation. In genre, Qoheleth, like the standard version of Gilgamesh, is a pseudo-autobiography of a king. The book is dominated by the learned and experienced king.

AUTHORSHIP, DATE, SOCIAL LOCATION, AND INTEGRITY

The author of Qoheleth has no interest in giving us his name or biographical details, for he wants to create another identity—the legendary king (Solomon, though not named), who, on the basis of what he has seen, can teach wisdom to the reader. Scholars have proposed dates of composition ranging from the tenth century (in the assumption that Solomon wrote it) down to the first century

B.C.E. In the absence of historical references in the book, the best clue is its language. In the typology of the Hebrew language the book is postexilic. Two Persian loanwords (*pardēs*, "park," 2:5, cf. English "paradise," and *pitgām*, "sentence," 8:11) plus a large number of Aramaisms (Aramaic was the business language in the postexilic period) suggest the Persian period (539–331 B.C.E.). One particularly useful clue is the verb *šlṭ*, which in Qoheleth has the legal sense "to have right, power" regarding inheritances and assets. It occurs in 2:19, 5:18 (EV 19), and the related nouns occur, "proprietor" in 7:19, 8:9 and "authority, right," in 8:4, 6. After the Persian period, however, *šlṭ* loses its legal sense and means only "to rule, to have dominion." Linguistic evidence, therefore, suggests the Persian period, more specifically a date between 450–350 B.C.E., which is slightly earlier than the modern consensus.[4]

What is the author's social location or milieu? One of the main topics of the book is money and the economy (more on this to come), so it is reasonable to infer the author was an upper-class person with enough income, disposable wealth, and property to know and be personally affected by the economic system. J. Kugel infers that he belonged to a class of financial "high-rollers," above making small loans to needy farmers; his money was *invested;* he envies the worker's untroubled sleep (5:12); "the one phenomenon that truly seems to bring tears to his eyes is not poverty so much as the fall from riches, the fate of one whose father has lost the family fortune (5:12-17) or one who amasses wealth only to see it taken away by another."[5] C. L. Seow has compiled evidence about the economy in the Persian or Achaeminid Empire (539–333 B.C.E.), in which Judah was a satrapy. A new feature of the period was the important role of money, rather than property, cattle, or precious metal weighed out for individual transactions. To facilitate collecting taxes and stimulate trade, the government began to mint coins and standardize currency. Coins and standardized currency were already known, but the scale of their use and the resulting surge of activity around taxes, wages, rent, loans, fines, inherited goods, and prices of goods were unprecedented. Money was no longer a convenient medium of exchange but a commodity.[6] Qoheleth's terminology reflects the increased importance of money and commerce: beside the familiar terms *kesep*, "money," *'ošer*, "wealth," and *naḥălâ*, "inheritance," one finds *yitrôn*, "surplus, gain," *'inyān*, "preoccupation, venture, business," *ḥēleq*, "lot, portion." Qoheleth "reflects a monetary and commercial economy, an environment that is different from the largely subsistence agrarian culture of preexilic Judah. In the fifth century, commerce was democratized and privatized; it was no longer primarily a royal enterprise."[7]

Scholars once assumed that the high taxes of the Persian Empire made for a stagnant economy, but new evidence suggests otherwise. The economy was healthy and afforded many opportunities for the alert entrepreneur. Opportunity and credit were not available to all equally, however. Smallholders had to pay rents and taxes with what they had, and were liable to foreclosure. Thus there was opportunity for some and danger for others. Qoheleth paints a picture of a society in which people fear for their future, for tomorrow is uncertain. Economics becomes a metaphor for human life. Sudden gains and sudden losses symbolize the larger disjunction between an act and its consequence; arbitrary and unquestionable actions of the powerful and of officials mirror the inscrutability of divine governance; anxious planning and hard work do not earn people much compensation in the form of happiness. The social location and date of the book help the reader understand the author's message.

The last preliminary question concerns the integrity of the book. Is it whole and entire from one author, or have later "more orthodox" editors and copyists added material? Several scholars attribute "inconsistencies" in the book to different authors or stages in the author's life, but such reconstructions have found few followers. Today, most commentators are inclined to treat the book as a literary unity, though most regard 12:9-14 (or vv. 12-14) as a correcting, "orthodox" addition to make the whole acceptable.

OUTLINE

There is no consensus on the outline of the book, but some agreement on the demarcation of many of its units. The outline here is minimalist and attempts to stay with the consensus.

1:2-3	Frame (cf. 12:8)
1:4-11	Cosmology: change, duration, and forgetting
1:12–2:26	I the king and the results of my search
3:1-22	Times are predetermined, fooling the human mind

4:1-16	Striving leaves one unsatisfied
4:17–5:6 (EV 5:1-7)	Advice on religious duties
5:7–6:9 (EV 5:8–6:9)	Enjoy life, avoid greed
6:10–7:14	Despite wise sayings, no one knows what is good
7:15-29	Righteousness and justice elude us
8:1-17	An arbitrary world
9:1-10	The same fate comes to all; enjoy today
9:11–10:15	Life is risk
10:16–11:6	How to live with political and economic risks
11:7–12:8	Poem on old age and death
12:8	Frame (cf. 1:2-3).

Two other outlines deserve mention. A. G. Wright's is based on key words and on numerology and has influenced modern scholarship:

I. Qoheleth's Investigation of Life and His Advice (1:1–6:9)
  A. Introduction (1:1-18)
  B. A Report of His Investigations and Advice (2:1–6:9)
II. The Inadequacy of Other Advice and of Our Knowledge of the Future (6:10–12:4)
  A. Introduction (6:10-12)
  B. The Development of the Two Topics (7:1–11:6)
    a. No One Can Find Out What Is Good to Do (7:1–8:17)
    b. No One Knows the Future (9:1–11:6)
  C. Conclusion (11:7–12:14)[8]

The other is by N. Lohfink, who views the book as chiastic in structure:

1:2-3	Frame
1:4-11	Cosmology (poem)
1:12–3:15	Anthropology
3:16–4:16	Critique of society I
5:1-7	Critique of religion (poem)
5:8–6:10	Critique of society II
6:11–9:6	Critique of prevailing wisdom
9:7–12:7	Ethics (at end, the poem)
12:8	Frame[9]

102

THE ARGUMENT OF THE BOOK

The framing verses, "Vanity of vanities" (1:2-3 and 12:8), describe everything as *hebel,* "breath." *Hebel* characterizes some aspects of life as insubstantial and transient, and other aspects as wrong or repugnant. To translate every occurrence "absurd" (in a modern existential sense) is too sweeping; the word is used in different senses.

Section 1:4-11 is a cosmology, a view of the "universe" as a stage for the human race. Ancient philosophies often presupposed a cosmology, which served as a basis for their ethics. The movement of the cosmos (symbolized by the constantly circulating air and water) is renewed (vv. 4b-7) but not the human race that lives in it (v. 4a). Indeed, human beings are deceived by the shortness of their life and the cyclic and predetermined course of events (vv. 8-11). Verse 8 is the transition from the impersonal universe to human beings. It is best translated not "all *things* are wearisome" (NRSV) but "all *words*[10] are wearying; / a human being cannot express it"; that is, human intelligence cannot fathom and human words cannot express the nature of reality. There is a misalignment between reality and the mind. The same sentiment, and indeed the same rhythm of determined event and human ignorance, will be stated again later in the book: "[God] has made everything suitable for its time; moreover he has put a sense of past and future into their minds, yet they cannot find out what God has done from the beginning to the end" (3:11). What the prologue states as true in cosmic language will be reaffirmed in the course of the book in terms of human experience.

The king now makes his appearance (1:12–2:26), explaining how he has come to know personally what the cosmology has just stated. Using a self-presentation formula common in royal inscriptions, he begins, "I am Qoheleth. I have been a king over Israel in Jerusalem" (1:12 my translation). Like the kings of those inscriptions, he summarizes his achievements, focusing on his building projects and acquisition of gold and silver, and compares himself with his predecessors.[11] Qoheleth departs from those boasts of human achievement, however, by asserting that death makes all such accomplishments vain; death comes to a wise king as surely as to a fool (2:12-17). Like the legendary king Gilgamesh, this king has learned that, despite his grand achievements, death is the end for everyone.[12] This section (1:12–2:26) has a carefully articulated structure.

1:12–2:3	Introduction
2:4-11	My achievements as a king are unparalleled, but all of it is vanity (the phrase "works of my hands" opens and closes the section, v. 4 and v. 11).
2:12-17	Death comes to all; hence all is vanity. The translation of 12 is controverted (literally, "what is the person who comes after the king?") and is best rendered: "Who is the person who will come after me? Shall he control what has already been achieved?" The meaning: when I die, I cannot even control who gets my wealth.[13]
2:18-23	This section matches 2:4-11 in expressing the futility of human toil (the root 'ml, "toil," occurs ten times in six verses!).
2:24-26	Conclusion. Enjoy yourself, for that is from the hand of God.

The brief counsel in 2:24-26, "Enjoy yourself!" may seem a strange conclusion to the lengthy and sober royal reflection. It is, however, the advice that Gilgamesh got from the tavern-keeper Siduri (discussed under "Genre") and will appear again and again in the book (3:12-13, 22; 5:17-18 [EV 5:18-19]; 8:15; 9:7-10; 11:9-10). So important a passage is worth translating and examining in detail.

> There is nothing worthwhile for a person but to eat and drink and enjoy the benefit of his toil. Yes, I have seen that this is the gift of God. For who can eat and who can enjoy without him? For to the person with whom God is pleased he gives wisdom and knowledge and joy, but to the one who misses he gives a preoccupation with gathering and accumulating so as to give it to the one with whom God is pleased. This too is vanity and a pursuit of wind. (my translation)

It is God's gift that people enjoy ("eat and drink") the present moment. Why? Possessing and enjoying the fruits of one's toil is not in human beings' hands but God's. Some people are inexplicably favored by God with the ability to enjoy what they have, others are not. Therefore, seize the day! Some translations take the subjects in verse 26 in a moral sense, "the one who pleases [God]" and "the sinner," but the terms are better rendered in a nonmoral sense, the person with whom God happens to be pleased (inexplicably to

104

human beings) and the one with whom God is (inexplicably to human beings) not pleased.

The next two sections, chapters 3 and 4, further develop the views stated "cosmically" in 1:4-11 and "autobiographically" in 1:12-26: human beings, being mortal, cannot adequately know the universe nor can they control their destinies; it is "wisdom" to accept enjoyment as a gift. Chapter 3 expands on the first idea—we do not adequately know or control our reality. Chapter 4 develops the second idea, enjoy the present. Chapters 3 and 4 end the first section in the book, for chapter 5 shifts the subject to a new topic, religious conduct.

Chapter 3 is the most quoted chapter in Qoheleth, "For everything there is a season, and a time for every matter under heaven: A time to be born, and a time to die . . . " Contrary to the popular interpretation that there is a right moment for people to do things, verses 2-8 (fourteen antithetical "times") mean just the reverse: all moments are in the hands of God, who does them in a rhythm that is beyond human calculation. Verse 9 asks the question that inevitably arises from the fact that all moments are determined by God: what good is human toil? Human beings will never recognize the uselessness of their anxious toil, however, because of an epistemological defect: "[God] has made everything suitable for its time; moreover he has put a sense of past and future into their minds, yet they cannot find out what God has done from the beginning to the end" (3:11). Because human history is predetermined (3:2-8) and because human knowledge is inadequate, it is no wonder that Qoheleth advises enjoyment: "I know that there is nothing worthwhile for them but to rejoice and enjoy while they live" (v. 12). Many commentators take verses 16-22 as a separate piece, but it belongs to verses 1-15, for it restates the earlier observation of determined times for a new context: "God will judge the righteous and the wicked, for he has appointed *a time* for every matter" (= 3:1). The verse does not say there will be a future divine judgment but simply asserts that, given the recurrence of "times," judgment of evil will eventually take place. Verses 18-21 restate the dominance of divinely assigned "times" by asserting human beings have no advantage over animals, for all die. Hence, enjoy the present moment (v. 22).

Chapter 4:1-16 contains several so-called *ṭôb* or "better-than" sayings, "X is better ["more good"] than Y," which are common in Egyptian and biblical wisdom literature (e.g., Qoh 7:1-12; Prov

15:16-17; 16:8; 28:6; Sir 29:22; 30:14). "Better-than" sayings purport to say that one thing is better than another in view of a third value, for example, "Better a dinner of vegetables where love is than a fatted ox and hatred with it." The *ṭôb*-sayings are somewhat ironic in the present context, however, for the book has already said several times how little we know and that there is nothing "more good" than simply accepting without question the present moment.

Most scholars recognize in 4:17–5:6 (EV 5:1-7) not only a discrete unit but also a new section in the book. Qoheleth has portrayed God up to this point quite differently from other biblical books. God is seen primarily as the author of an inscrutable divine order, which human beings know only in the activation of its individual moments. These counsels about dealing with God are, therefore, not surprising. Qoheleth's God seems more active with regard to human beings outside the religious precincts than inside. People find God in the joy of their work (3:12-13, 22; 5:17-18 [EV 5:18-19]; 8:15; 9:7-10; 11:9-10).

The next section (5:7–6:9 [EV 5:8–6:9]) can be shown to be a literary unit by its chiastic structure, which has been noted by D. C. Fredericks.[14] The outline is particularly valuable in that it provides an objective guide to Qoheleth's thought. The basic ideas of this section have appeared earlier, but the chiasm puts them in a fresh setting.

A 5:7-11 (EV 8-12)	*A' 6:7-9*
the poor (v. 7)	the afflicted (v. 8)
not satisfied (v. 9)	not satisfied (v. 7)
what accomplishment (v. 10)	what advantage (v. 8)
seeing of their eyes (v. 10)	seeing of eyes (v. 9)
B 5:12-16 (EV 13-17)	*B' 6:3-6*
he sired a son (v. 13)[15]	he sires a hundred (v. 3)
going as he came (v. 14)	he came . . . he went (v. 4)
he eats in darkness (v. 16)	he goes in darkness (v. 4)
C 5:17-18 (EV 18-19)	*C' 6:1-12*
good (v. 17)	evil (v. 1)
God has given (v. 18)	God gives (v. 2)
this is a gift (v. 20)	This is a sickness (v. 2)

D 5:19 (EV 20)
must not remember much
God preoccupies-responds with joy in the heart.

Section D is the center of the chiasm; sections ABC of the chiasm lead to it and sections A'B'C' away from it. The first section (A) lists people who cannot be satisfied (though the text is unclear). Section B gives an example of a person whose son could not enjoy his goods. Section C tells what is good. Section D gives the main point. Section C' gives an example of what is bad, and section B' gives another example of a person whose descendants cannot enjoy their inheritance. With section A the whole essay comes full circle with the restatement of the theme of dissatisfaction.

The next section is 6:10–8:17. Lohfink interprets the entire unit as a critical review of old proverbial wisdom and would even extend the section to 9:6. There are several indications of organization such as the fourfold repetition of the phrase "[not] find out," which suggests four sections (7:1-14; 7:15-24; 7:25-29; 8:1-17), and the recurrence of the phrase "I have observed." It is not always easy, however, to decide if these markers are structurally significant.

In 6:10–7:14, a series of maxims (7:1-12) is framed by two statements of the determination of all events (6:10-12 and 7:13-14). The preface is 6:10-12: "What happens has already been designated and the course of human history is known; a person cannot dispute with the one who is stronger than he is. The more words, the more vanity" (my translation). In view of the preface, how can the reader take the "words" or aphorisms that follow in 7:1-12 without a grain of salt? The conclusion seems to be that human words provide only partial guidance.

The next section (7:15-29) states that one should not too quickly trust in one's righteousness (vv. 15-20), for righteousness and its correlative, wisdom, are elusive. The idea is developed by remarks that seem at first sight to be extremely misogynic: "I found more bitter than death the woman who is a trap, whose heart is snares and nets, whose hands are fetters; one with whom God is pleased escapes her, but the one who misses is taken by her" (v. 26, my translation). The verse must refer to folly, who is personified in Proverbs 1–9 as a *femme fatale*, trapping the young man in her nets. Qoheleth here says that he earnestly sought wisdom, which can be personified as an attractive woman. Her literary foil is Woman Folly, and Qoheleth confesses that he has sometimes fallen into her traps (see Prov 5; 6:20-35; 7).

The passage is therefore not misogynic but simply a statement that folly is an ever-present danger, and escaping it depends on God's favor. Verse 28b has added to the confusion: "One man among a thousand I found, but a woman among all these I have not found."

Verse 28 is a problem that puzzles the most astute commentator, and was perhaps added by a scribe.[16]

Chapter 8 especially verses 1-8, is a difficult passage and will not be discussed here.

The next large section in the book, in the opinion of many scholars, is 9:1–12:8.[17] Within this large section, 9:1-10 is a unit, for the theme of verses 1-6 (the same fate for all living creatures) prepares for the message in verses 7-10, "Gather ye rosebuds while ye may." The next unit is made up of 9:11–10:15, consisting of three subunits, each introduced by "I have seen-observed" (9:11-12; 9:13–10:4; 10:5-15). Traditional wisdom literature set great store by the inherent connection between people's actions and the consequences resulting from them. Virtuous behavior produces prosperity, and wicked behavior brings trouble. Not so, says Qoheleth. On the basis of *my* experience ("*I* have observed"), the race is not won by the swift nor the battle by the strong, but a "time" befalls us all. The traditional translation "time and chance" is a hendiadys (two words signifying one idea).[18] "Time" has the meaning it has in 3:1-11: "For everything there is a season, and a *time* for every matter under heaven." A little story illustrates the disconnection of deed and result: "There was a little city with few people in it. A great king came against it and besieged it, building great siegeworks against it. Now there was found in it a poor wise man, and he by his wisdom delivered the city. Yet no one remembered that poor man" (9:14-15). One must learn to live in an uncertain universe, and live with the risks. The rest of the section lists further examples of acts that do not automatically generate expected consequences (10:5-7). Chapter 10:8-11 mentions risks; accidents can happen. The verbs are best translated as modals, "Whoever digs a pit *may* fall into it, and whoever digs through a wall *may* be bitten by a snake" (10:8). Yet even in a chance-dominated universe, there is *some* advantage in wisdom (10:12-15). What is the advantage? The wise win themselves favor (10:12*a*) and their speech does not land them in the kind of trouble fools get themselves into (10:12*b*-15). This is a far cry from the lofty claims of traditional wisdom!

Chapters 10:16–11:6 are a loose collection of individual items, continuing from the foregoing unit (9:11–10:15) the theme of living with risks. The unit changes grammatical person, going from reflection in the third person to direct address of the reader in the second person. The unit contains formal indications that the piece is coherent and unified: in 11:6 "in the morning" reprises 10:16 "in the morning"; in 11:6, "slackness of hand" reprises "slackness of hands" in 10:18. One of the famous but puzzling lines in Qoheleth is 11:1, "Send out your bread upon the waters; / for after many days you will get it back." The verse in recent years has been interpreted as an exhortation to take risks in business ("bread" is money) or to be so recklessly generous as to throw bread (flat round loaves) upon waters that will soak and sink it. The second interpretation—Be generous!—has ancient support.

The final unit, 11:7–12:7, concerns youth and old age, and includes the haunting poem on old age (12:1-7). Though a few scholars differ on the starting point of the section, 11:7 commandingly establishes the image of light that continues throughout. The first part (11:7-10) urges the youth to look joyfully on the light before the darkness comes; the second part (12:1-8) tells what happens when the light has faded and the darkness has come.

We should note the important place the poem occupies in the structure of the book, for it reprises the opening cosmology (1:4-11). Both the opening and closing poems are concerned with vulnerable and uncomprehending human beings. The cosmology of chapter 1 opens with the passing away of a human generation (v. 4), and verses 8-11 speak of people's inability to understand their mortality within the perennial rhythm of the universe. The poem on old age and death (12:1-7) also includes cosmic elements, for the darkening of the heavens (12:2) forms the backdrop of the collapse of a household and the death and funeral of its owner. In particular, 12:5-6 reprise words in 1:4-6 (using some of them in a new way): *hālak*, "to go" in its sense of pass away, die; *sābab*, "turns around"; "go about (in procession)," the phrase *hārûaḥ tāšûb*, "the breath-wind (re)turns," *'ôlām*, "eternity," and earth as the unvarying foundation of all things. The final verse of the body of the book, 12:8, "Vanity of vanities, says Qoheleth, all is vanity" reprises the first verses (1:2-3). At the end of the book, its great paradox finds memorable expression: enjoy life now *because* life is beyond your knowledge and control!

Having looked at the poem's placement in the book, a word needs to be said on the poem itself, which presents several difficulties. The first part (11:7-10) actually commands the youth (the typical recipient of wisdom instruction in antiquity) to *enjoy* life, "Follow the inclination of your heart and the desire of your eyes" (11:9*cd*). The phrase, "God will bring you into judgment" (11:9*f*) is sometimes regarded as a gloss by a scribe fearful of the command to enjoy, but there is no evidence it was added. It can mean that there will inevitably be a "time" for weeping (cf. 3:17) or that God will judge you for not enjoying the present.[19] The typical Qoheleth word *hebel*, "breath, vanity," occurs in 11:10, "for youth and black hair are *hebel*." Its meaning here has to be "fleeting, (like a) breath," showing the word has a variety of meanings in the book.

The controversies around 12:1-7 can be reduced to two: (1) is 12:1 to be translated "Remember the creator," or something else? (2) are verses 1-6 to be interpreted allegorically, literally, or figuratively? With regard to the first question, MT has "your creator,"[20] which is remarkably like the Hebrew for "your health" and "your cistern, pit." MT "your creator" makes the most sense in a book inculcating enjoyment of life as a gift of God (5:19), but there may be wordplay on death ("pit") or the cistern in 12:6.

The second question is more complicated, for it concerns the interpretation of the whole. An allegorical approach was taken by the targum, midrash, Talmud, and others: the decay of the house represents the decay of old age. The waning lights represent the parts of the face, the trembling guards and the bent strong men are the arms and legs, the grinders are the teeth, those who look out the windows are the eyes, the closing of the doors is the closing of ears, eyes, lips, the white almond tree blossoms represent gray hair. In response, one can concede that the topic of the poem is certainly human decline leading to death, but an exclusively allegorical interpretation slights the indisputable cosmic and universal dimension of the passage. The text as it now stands includes conventional descriptions of the unpleasantness and even horrors of old age (see 2 Sam 19:6 [EV 19:5]), which are combined with conventional descriptions of cosmic doom, such as one finds in eschatological texts.[21] Beginning in 12:1-2, "Remember your creator in the days of your youth, before the days of trouble come, and the years draw near . . . before the sun and the light and the moon and the stars are darkened . . . ," the mood becomes increasingly somber. Several dimensions (not just one person's old age) are skillfully blended: the collapse of a great and busy house, the decay (physical and emotional) of an old person, the decline of a town, and the cosmic collapse traditionally associated with definitive divine judgment. The verses bring to mind a funeral procession. The last words are "earth," which receives the dead body, and "God," to whom the breath returns (12:7). The end could not be more vividly sketched.

The human world disappears. Is this what is meant in the cosmology, "a generation goes" (1:4)?

The epilogue (12:9-14) is obviously an appendix, outside the framework of the book itself. It could have been written by Qoheleth himself,[22] but most take it as a note added by someone else to offer an explanation of a difficult book.

INTERPRETATIONS OF THE BOOK

The preceding section is a guide to the most significant texts of Qoheleth, but it does not provide a synthesis or overall interpretation. To assist in forming such a synthesis, several recent commentators are summarized or quoted here, so that the reader can react to them as well as to Qoheleth. In reading the commentators, note their assessment of Qoheleth's view of God, of the value of human work, whether they judge Qoheleth a pessimist or an optimist, how they translate *hebel,* and who or what they consider his conversation partner to be.

Walther Zimmerli, formerly Old Testament professor at Göttingen, was a pioneer in the modern theological rediscovery of wisdom literature. He published a concise theological commentary in 1962.[23] For Zimmerli, Qoheleth was engaged in a dialogue with the sages and their traditional wisdom, and was especially critical of those who taught that wisdom mediated between God and human beings. Qoheleth attacked wisdom's boast to give everything people need. He is no skeptic since he believes the world is the Lord's. Qoheleth's position is clearest in 8:16-17. At the center of his thinking is the "right moment" (a concern of traditional wisdom too), which people cannot know (3:1-15). The deeper meaning of our inability to gain mastery of time is that "God has done it all in such a way that people must fear him." Therefore, do not be overrighteous or wise. The book is not pessimistic, for it teaches that everything is in the hand of God.

J. L. Crenshaw is a specialist in wisdom literature. His *Ecclesiastes* reflects on the book:

> Life is profitless; totally absurd. This oppressive message lies at the heart of the Bible's strangest book. Enjoy life if you can, advises the author, for old age will soon overtake you. And even as you enjoy, know that the world is meaningless. Virtue does not bring reward. The deity stands distant, abandoning humanity to chance and

111

death. . . . Because death cancels every human achievement, Qoheleth concludes that life has no meaning. Death mocks personal
ambition and frugality. Qoheleth realizes that death grips some
people long before they actually die. These individuals may amass
fortunes but they cannot enjoy the benefits. Qoheleth considers them
less fortunate than stillborns, who at least enjoy rest. (pp. 23, 25-26)[24]

Norbert Lohfink uses philosophical language to summarize
Qoheleth:

Qoheleth analyzes human existence [German *Dasein*] as being *[Sein]*
in time, which is given only in the swiftly passing now and ends in
death for individuals. It may be experienced as chance. [Death] is
more than a sinking into oblivion, because in every instance it arises
out of the eternity of a world-transcending God who is behind every
event without exception. His action is total. He also judges wickedness. Human beings cannot fathom the activity of God, with the result
that he is experienced as mysterious and amoral. One knows, of
course, that there is an overall meaning, but one cannot "get at" it;
only God does. One can only entrust oneself to what comes to one at
every moment from God.[25]

Lohfink is critical of scholars who judge Qoheleth deviant on the
basis of a "biblical" theology derived from only a few biblical books:
"If someone, to protect the other books of the Bible (as is fashionable among exegetes), uses labels [for Qoheleth] like 'no personal
God,' 'denial of human freedom,' 'deviation from historical thinking,' 'lack of trust in life,' one runs away from the book's challenge
to thought, and is in danger of falsifying what one intends to defend"
(15-16).

Roland Murphy's *Ecclesiastes* attempts to overcome the disad-
vantages of summarizing an existential thinker like Qoheleth by
commenting on what he sees as Qoheleth's ten key ideas: vanity,
profit, portion, toil, joy, fear of God, wisdom, retribution, death, and
God.[26] To situate Qoheleth at the center of the Bible rather than at
its margins, Murphy criticizes H. Hertzberg's assessment that "the
book of Qoheleth, standing at the end of the Old Testament, is the
most staggering messianic prophecy to appear in the Old Testament." Hertzberg explains: "[The] Old Testament was here on the
point of running itself to death. Behind this total nothing from a
human point of view, the only possible help was the 'new creature'
of the New Testament."[27] Murphy prefers the words of Dietrich

Bonhoeffer, "It is only when one loves life and the earth so much that without them everything [would be gone,] that one [can] believe in the resurrection and a new world."[28]

Michael Fox comes to three main conclusions about Qoheleth's thought: (1) Qoheleth is chiefly concerned with the rationality of existence, which he denies by calling everything *hebel*, "breath, vanity"; (2) he does not attack wisdom, the wise, or the doctrines of wisdom literature but expresses his esteem for wisdom; (3) not finding meaning in the world, Qoheleth affirms the grasping of *inner experience*, emotional and intellectual, as the one domain of human freedom. Yet even this is not wholly satisfactory. Fox attempts to name the "contradictions" of Qoheleth and examine them rather than explain them away. The main "contradictions" are for him: toil is absurd and without profit, yet it provides the wealth that will provide joy; Qoheleth affirms and denies the possibility and the value of wisdom; life is unjust but God is just.[29]

The final commentator to be mentioned is Choon-Leong Seow. Aware of the danger of systematizing an experiential thinker, Seow paraphrases "the content" on pages 47-54 of his commentary, and then in a "theological anthropology" (a phrase that tries to capture both the theological and philosophical aspects of Qoheleth) he offers a synthesis (54-60). His final summary paragraph is printed here.

> In sum, Qohelet always begins his reflection with humanity and the human condition. He concludes at every turn that mortals are not in control of the things that happen in the world. They are not in control of their destiny. This is why Qohelet says that everything is *hebel*. He does not mean that everything is meaningless or insignificant, but that everything is beyond human apprehension and comprehension. But in thinking about humanity, Qohelet also speaks of God. People are caught in the situation where everything is *hebel*—in every sense of the word. God is transcendent and wholly other, but humanity is "on earth." Yet God is related to humanity, and God has given humanity the possibilities of each moment. Hence people must accept what happens, whether good or bad. They must respond spontaneously to life, even in the midst of uncertainties, and accept both the possibilities and limitations of their being human.

Obviously, the commentators here cited disagree about some of the main points in Qoheleth. One means of achieving a personal synthesis is to identify what you consider to be the key passages in Qoheleth and to use them as the basis of your synthesis.

RECOMMENDED READING

Commentaries

Crenshaw, James L. *Ecclesiastes*. Old Testament Library. Philadelphia: Westminster, 1987. Clear and erudite, with an emphasis on theological issues. Crenshaw stresses the skeptical and contrarian side of Qoheleth.

Fox, Michael V. *Qoheleth and His Contradictions*. Journal for the Study of the Old Testament—Supplement Series 71, Bible and Literature Series 18. Sheffield: Almond, 1989. In an original approach, Fox probes the contradictions of the book.

Gordis, Robert. *Koheleth: The Man and His World: A Study of Ecclesiastes*. 3rd ed. New York: Schocken, 1968. Excellent on background, sometimes explains too much by psychology.

Lohfink, Norbert. *Kohelet*. Neue Echter Bibel. Würzburg: Echter Verlag, 1980. Lohfink regards Qoheleth as less skeptical than most commentators. A rich and subtle commentary.

Murphy, Roland E. *Ecclesiastes*. Word Biblical Commentary 23. Dallas: Word, 1992. Learned, well balanced, and very accessible, Murphy's work fits Qoheleth into a broader context than many commentaries.

Seow, Choon-Leong. *Ecclesiastes*. Anchor Bible 18C. New York: Doubleday, 1997. Strong in the analysis of the language and in comparing similar literature, it never loses track of the message of the book. It is also accessible to the general reader.

Whybray, R. N. *Ecclesiastes*. New Century Bible Commentary. Grand Rapids: Eerdmans, 1989. Judicious and balanced.

Wright, Addison G., "Ecclesiastes," in *NJBC*, 489-95. Brief. Offers important suggestions about the structure.

CHAPTER 6

THE WISDOM OF
BEN SIRA (SIRACH)

The book is known under several names, the Wisdom of Ben Sira, Sirach, and Ecclesiasticus, the latter a shortened form of *liber ecclesiasticus*, "church book," from its frequent usage in the early church. By modern convention, Ben Sira (or Jesus Ben Sira) is used for the author and Sirach is used for the book. The book belongs to the Apocrypha, or Deuterocanonical books, that is, books that were not part of the Hebrew canon used by Jews and Protestant Christians but part of the canon that is used by the Orthodox and by Roman Catholics. There has been a revival of interest in Sirach not only for its own qualities but also for the window it opens into Palestinian Judaism of the second century B.C.E.

Sirach is an anthology of texts like Proverbs, not a work with a persistent logical thread like Job or Wisdom of Solomon. Hence, I will approach it like Proverbs; that is, I will provide some background information, comment on the genres within it, and then sample important texts. Sirach has a much more defined doctrine than Proverbs, however, which will be presented as the final part of my treatment.

DATE, TEXT, AUTHOR, AND SOCIAL LOCATION

Sirach is the only wisdom book that can be dated exactly. Jesus Ben Sira wrote his work in Hebrew sometime in the 180s B.C.E., after the death of the high priest Simon[1] and before the Maccabean-Seleucid conflict that broke out in 175 B.C.E., which he does not mention. As Ben Sira's grandson tells us in his prologue, he translated his grandfather's Hebrew into Greek in Alexandria in Egypt after 132 B.C.E. (= thirty-eighth year of the reign of Euergetes).

Since the Wisdom of Ben Sira did not become Jewish Scripture, the Hebrew text ceased to be copied and was effectively lost from about 400 to 1900 C.E. Church authors cite the grandson's Greek translation and some other versions. At the turn of the twentieth century, Hebrew fragments were discovered in a Cairo depository for worn-out manuscripts, and subsequently additional fragments were discovered at Qumran and at Masada. About two-thirds of the Hebrew text has been recovered. Even with the Hebrew, the textual situation is complicated. The original Hebrew of Ben Sira (= Hebrew I) is preserved in the fragments from Qumran and Masada and, indirectly, in the Greek of the critical edition edited by J. Ziegler (= Greek I). The Hebrew text suffered additions and rewritings even before the Christian period (= Hebrew II), which was translated rather freely into Greek (= Greek II) and Syriac. In short, Sirach exists in both a short text (reckoned as more original) and in a long text (reckoned as less original). Because of the confused textual history, there are variations in the verse numbers of modern translations. Readers should use only translations of Sirach that have been made since the 1970s.

Sirach 50:27 gives us the name of the author, "Teachings for understanding and knowledge I have written in this book, Jesus (= Hebrew Yeshua) Son of Eleazar, son of Sira, of Jerusalem, whose mind poured forth wisdom." This little note breaks with the venerable biblical custom of anonymous authorship. Ben Sira is the only wisdom author whose name we know. From 38:24–39:11 we learn of Ben Sira's keen sense of his craft as sage, for after contrasting it with other crafts (39:24-34), he exclaims, "How different the one who devotes himself / to the study of the law of the Most High!" (38:34cd). A sage studies the Scriptures, ponders proverbs, advises rulers, travels to foreign lands, all the while praying to God for wisdom, "If he lives long, he will leave a name greater than a thousand" (39:1-11). Did Ben Sira operate alone or did he function within a recognized institution? His autobiographical poem gives a hint: "Draw near to me, you who are uneducated, / and lodge in the house of instruction *[bêt midraš]* " (51:23). Unfortunately, it is not clear whether the "house of instruction" refers to a real school or is a metaphor for discipleship. What is clear is that Ben Sira has a clear sense of his distinct vocation as a scholar, an intellectual able to address rulers and comment authoritatively on personal, familial, and national issues and ethics, and also to speak for God (39:1-11). Throughout his book he confidently invokes the ancient wisdom tradition, offers prophetic critique (cf. 24:33), retells the historical traditions (chaps. 44–50), and interprets the Law (chap. 24).

Scholars dispute how much influence Hellenistic culture exerted on Ben Sira. Hellenistic culture was introduced to the East by the all-conquering Alexander of Macedon in 356–323 B.C.E. Alexander broke down national, linguistic, and cultural boundaries and inaugurated with full deliberateness a cosmopolitan culture in the East. An important strand in the new culture was Stoicism, a philosophy teaching that the universe was ruled by the divine Logos (word, rationality), which was immanent within it, and that human beings had the duty of conforming themselves to nature and to reason as reflections of the Logos. In Stoicism, wisdom consists in the harmony of the individual with the whole. The universal perspective of Stoicism (and of the Hellenistic culture generally) challenged the Jewish sense of election and of its God who utterly transcended the world. Traces of Stoicism have been discerned in Sirach, in his ideal of human dignity (41:14–42:8), in his ideal of the unity of the world (43:27), and of the human race (36:1-4, 22).[2] Another philosophical current that has been discerned in Sirach is Epicureanism, which strove for a life ruled by reason, marked by equilibrium within, free of bodily pain and inner disquiet. Echoes of Epicureanism have been perceived in Sirach 14:11-16; 30:21-25; 31:27-29).[3] Some scholars see Ben Sira as engaged in a polemic with these new ideas, whereas others see him as a traditionalist, interested only in revitalizing the national writings.

OUTLINE

Sirach is a vast collection of essays, ethical teachings, reflections about wisdom and Judaism. There is no general plan within which the essays find their place. Moral teachings on daily life are mingled with more speculative considerations on wisdom and the human condition from a Jewish perspective. Themes appear, vanish, and return in later chapters. If anything, the connection between the sections is by catchword or by association of ideas. It is difficult to judge the boundaries of many of the essays, and there is thus considerable variation in the outlines proposed by commentators. Minissale, for example, sees one hundred thirty-one units, whereas Skehan and Di Lella find only sixty-three.[4] Perhaps the most efficient initial approach to the huge anthology is to borrow the outline (with only one change: shifting no. 50 to part VIII) of Skehan and Di Lella. Admittedly, its divisions are quite broad here and there, but it has the virtue of brevity. It also correctly judges the wisdom poems in the book to be introductions to sections.

119

56. The Northern Kingdom: 58. Josiah and the Prophets:
    Elijah and Elisha   Heroes Early and Late
    (47:23–48:15d)   (49:1-16)
57. Judah: Hezekiah and Isaiah 59. Simeon, Son of Jochanan
    (48:15e-25)   (50:1-24)

Conclusion (50:25–51:30)

60. Judah's Neighbors; Postscript to the Book (50:25-29)
61. Ben Sira's Prayer (51:1-12)
62. Hymn of Praise from the Time of Ben Sira (51:12 i-xvi)
63. Autobiographical Poem on Wisdom (51:13-30)

KEY PASSAGES

As the outline indicates, each of the eight parts of Sirach begins with a poem on wisdom. This section will comment on several of the more important passages in the book.

Chapter 1:1-10 opens the entire book, considering wisdom from three points of view: (1) as a quality of God, belonging to his nature, which is shown by the rhetorical questions in verse 6; (2) as the order within the world, hidden yet made known by God, which human beings cannot fathom; (3) as a divine gift, given by God to his friends, especially to the people of Israel.

The poem illustrates the essay style of Ben Sira, in which he uses the traditional bicolon (the basic building block of Hebrew poetry) to construct an essay. The reader has to discover the logic that makes the verses a coherent poem. The logic of this poem is not difficult, though it may escape a first-time reader of Sirach. Verse 1 is the thesis—wisdom is *with* God. In verses 2-3 wisdom is described as the order of the world,[5] which no one but God knows, hence the rhetorical questions, "Who can count them? . . . Who can search them out?" The world was definitively established in all its operations on the day of creation (vv. 4-9). It should be noted that evolutionary development from simple to more complex states, which the modern West takes for granted in thinking about the world, is foreign to ancient cosmology; on the day of creation the world was simply laid out as it was always to be. The world is wholly oriented toward the divine world; it is theocentric. It is wisdom to know one's place in the universe that the gods (or God) made *for themselves* (or *Godself*). Wisdom teaches one's place in the universe; to revere God in this theocentric world is what Sirach means by "fear of the Lord," which will be the topic of the next poem in verses 11-30. "Fear of the Lord" is better translated "revering God (or Yahweh)," for it is less an emotion than a conviction to fulfill one's duties to God. Because "fear of the Lord" is such a venerable phrase, we will often use it rather than "revering the Lord" in this chapter.

The next poem, 1:11-30, is also programmatic for the book. Its goal is to explain "fear of the Lord," as Ben Sira understands it, and to show its attractiveness and its relation to wisdom. Wisdom and fear of the Lord are central to Sirach's thought. The poem is an acrostic; that is, it has twenty-two lines, which is the number of the consonants in the Hebrew alphabet. Sometimes each line of an acrostic poem began with a successive consonant; it is impossible to tell what kind of acrostic this poem is, for the Hebrew is not preserved. It forms an *inclusio* with the closing poem of the book, also an acrostic, in 51:13-30.

The structure of the poem is visible, even without the original Hebrew.

I. 11-13 Fear of the Lord and its gifts
    14-20 Fear of the Lord as the *beginning* (v. 14a), *fullness* (v. 16a),
    crown (v. 18a), and *root* (v. 20a) of wisdom
II.[6] 22-29 The obstacles to acquiring fear of the Lord, impatience
    and hypocrisy, and the means to it, obedience and discipline
    30 Consequences of rejecting fear of the Lord.

The poem begins and ends with the phrase "fear of the Lord," forming an *inclusio*. "Fear of the Lord" occurs twelve times, apparently a significant number, for it is the number of the tribes of Israel and the months of the year. The closing three bicola in verse 30 reverse the opening three bicola in verses 11-13: exalting oneself instead of allowing wisdom to do it (v. 11) ends in disgrace. In verses 14-20, the descriptions are paired, beginning and completion (= end), crown and root—merisms that express totality.[7] In sum, revering Yahweh is the fundamental attitude one needs to live wisely and thus enjoy all the good things of life.

Having proposed his basic teachings on wisdom and fear of the Lord in the early chapters of the book, Ben Sira in 15:11-20 can become more philosophical and less "biblical," tackling the issue of free will. Normally, the Bible simply affirms both divine sovereignty and human freedom without regarding the point as a philosophical "problem," but here the author engages in philosophical discourse. Verses 11-12 cite popular statements that divine power does away with the human capacity to act freely. Nonsense, says Ben Sira. God abhors evil and has no need of it. "It was he who created humankind in the beginning, / and he left them in the power of their own free choice [yēṣer]. / If you choose, you can keep the commandments, / and to act faithfully is a matter of your own choice" (vv. 14-15). The italicized word yēṣer (here and in 27:6b) means "disposition, tendency," and was important in rabbinic thought in the phrase yēṣer hārā ', "evil inclination." The concept can be traced back to Genesis 8:21 and 6:5, "The LORD saw . . . that every inclination [yēṣer] of the thoughts of their hearts was only evil continually." For Sirach, the disposition is neutral, approximately equal to free will. Characteristically, Ben Sira answers the objections in verses 11-12 by appealing to experience (you have the ability to keep the commandments) and, much more important, by an appeal to the character of God. God is not the sort of divinity who must employ evil to govern (vv. 11b, 12b, 13); he has endowed human beings with the power of choice (yēṣer, vv. 14-17). Paradoxically, divine wisdom and power require that human beings be free (vv. 18-20). Later in the book, Ben Sira will give another answer to the same problem of evil (33:14-15)—God has created things in pairs: "Good is the opposite of evil, / and life the opposite of death; / so the sinner is the opposite of the godly. / Look at all the works of the Most High; / they come in pairs, one the opposite of the other." The immediately following section, 16:1-23, which is concerned with the topic of the correspondence between human action and divine response, is judged by some commentators a continuation of our poem. Whether or not it is a part in the strict sense, it shows the close thematic connection of adjacent sections that characterizes much of Sirach.

An example of a long and unified composition is the poem on creation in 16:24–18:14, which many regard as one poem, though some judge that it is merely a section made up of distinct poems on related themes. I presume that it is one poem and examine its logic. Chapter 16:24-25 begins with an invitation such as are found in the instructions in Proverbs 1–9 (1:8-9; 3:1; 4:1; 6:1; and so on), then rehearses the creation account in Genesis 1. Sirach 16:26-30 narrates the works of the first six days (Gen 1:1-25), and 17:1-14 narrates Genesis 1:26–2:3. With 17:6, however, the account begins to go beyond Genesis 1. Verses 6-7 allude to the story of the man and the woman (Gen 2:4a–3:24; cf. "good and evil" in 17:7b) and 17:8-13 leaves Genesis entirely, as it refers to the Sinai covenant (Exodus 19–24), in which God "established with them an eternal covenant" and "said to them, 'Beware of all evil,' / And he gave commandment to each of them concerning the neighbor" (17:12a, 14). Following the creation of the human race (and Israel) as moral and responsible, 17:15-24 portrays God as responsive to every human action, rewarding or punishing them with perfect exactness. Verses 25-27 logically follow the depiction of human beings as moral agents and God as guarantor of morality, for it is a call to conversion, "Turn back to the Lord and forsake your sins" (v. 25). Ben Sira underlines God's mercy ("How great is the mercy of the Lord," v. 29), which is another one of his innovations as a wisdom writer. The next section (18:1-14), presuming that the audience has decided to turn to the Lord, provides a hymn to God's majesty, which expresses gratitude for divine mercy, awareness of human fragility, and a statement of the rhythm of sin and forgiveness that marks the life of human beings with God. Such is the logic of this poem.

The most famous poem in the entire book is chapter 24. Its place at the center of Sirach and in the biblical development of wisdom demands that it be given a close reading. As we have seen, each part of the first half of Sirach opened with a poem on wisdom (1:1-10; 4:11-19; 6:18-37; 14:20–15:10), and chapter 24, advancing beyond them, opens the second half. Previous poems, to be sure, personified wisdom as a beloved object of human affections (teacher, mother, and wife), but their focus was on human beings. In chapter 24, personified Wisdom holds center stage from the beginning; only at the very end does the sage enter as her modest servant (vv. 30-34). Chapter 24 alludes to the great wisdom poem in Proverbs 8 by keeping to the same number of lines (thirty-five) and by explicitly citing in v. 9 Proverbs 8:22 ("The LORD created me at the beginning of his work, / the first of his acts of long ago"). It also alludes to Proverbs 9 by its invitation to a banquet in verses 19-23. The poem therefore consciously develops the concept of wisdom that had been handed down in earlier tradition.

The scene is a solemn liturgy celebrated in the Temple, for Wisdom speaks "in the midst of her people" and "in the assembly of the Most High" (vv. 1-2). The liturgy joins heaven and earth (cf. Isaiah 6). In twenty-two verses (vv. 3-22, acrostic form), Wisdom tells of her origin and history and renews the invitation she always holds out to the human race. The structure of verses 1-34 is in seven parts.

1. Vv. 1-2	Introduction of personified Wisdom
2. 3-6	Wisdom in creation
3. 7-11	Her dwelling in Israel
4. 12-17	Her praise using comparisons taken from the plant world
5. 18-21	Invitation to her banquet
6. 22-29	Identification of Wisdom with the Law given to Israel
7. 30-34	The vocation of Ben Sira as disciple and teacher of wisdom.

Three points deserve comment. First, more so than in Proverbs, the personification of wisdom is a literary representation of the word of God. Wisdom "came forth from the mouth of the Most High" (v. 3a), that is, she is God's word. Word is how God's wisdom primarily appears, and it is manifested both in creation and in the law. Word and wisdom are combined in the New Testament as well, most memorably in the first chapter of John's Gospel, "In the beginning was the Word," evoking both Proverbs 8:22 ("beginning") and Genesis 1:1-3 ("beginning," "God *said*"). Second, Wisdom is universal ("over every people and nation I have held sway") and active in human history, but explicitly active in the history of Israel, where she has taken up residence in the Temple (v. 4, "pillar of cloud"; v. 8, "tent"; and the implicit references to the Exodus in vv. 7-12). The relationship of wisdom to worship, cosmos, and history will appear again as a central theme in the Praise of the Ancestors in chapters 42:15–50:24. Third, the well-known identification of wisdom and the Torah in verse 23, "All this is the book of the covenant of the Most High God, / the law that Moses commanded us," should not be interpreted in a mechanical fashion, as a logical identification of two previously separate entities. Rather, Ben Sira "recognizes in biblical revelation the best expression of divine wisdom."[8]

The last great section of Sirach is 42:15–50:1-24, which leaves behind the moral teaching of earlier sections to praise the wisdom of God manifested in nature (42:15–43:33) and in the history of Israel (44:1–50:24).

The long poem on creation (42:15–43:33) belongs to the final section on the history of Israel ("Let us now praise famous men"), for the Bible does not share the modern Western sharp dichotomy between nature and history.[9] The universe depends on God's creative word, which is the expression of God's wisdom; the world is unified and functions coherently. The remarkable harmony of the world in the poem is perhaps the influence of Stoicism, according to which the universe is ruled by the immanent divine Logos or Word and the human race is invited to join that harmony. The phrase "He is the All" (v. 27) occurs in the famous Stoic "Hymn to Zeus," though Ben Sira distances himself from Stoic pantheism by affirming in the very next verse that God "is greater than all his works." The creation poem in Sirach begins with the author acknowledging his limits in giving praise (42:15-17) and focusing on the grandeur (vv. 18-21) and intrinsic goodness (vv. 22-25) of creation. Chapter 43 is an orderly listing of wonders in the heavens (vv. 1-12), meteorological activity (vv. 13-22), and wonders in the sea (vv. 23-26). The "natural" wonders are described in their effect upon human beings, for the human race is a constituent part of the biblical universe.

After 42:15–44:33 praises divine wisdom manifesting itself in the beautifully active universe, chapters 44–50 praise divine wisdom manifesting itself in human history. The chapters have long been neglected, but now the genre, structure, and purpose are the object of much study. The encomium, a Hellenistic genre, along with Hellenistic historiography, has influenced Ben Sira in writing these chapters, though without in any way diminishing his originality. Ben Sira also draws on the entire Bible, though his essay is best understood within biblical wisdom literature, especially as he has sketched it in chapter 24—glory as presence.[10]

The structure of chapters 44–50 is more complex than a series of sketches of heroes. Following an introduction (44:1-15), the history falls into three parts: (1) the period when the covenants were established (44:16–45:25; the Hebrew word for covenant [bĕrît] occurs seven times);[11] (2) the period of the kings and their kingdoms (46:13–49:10); (3) the Second Temple period after the exile (49:14–50:24). The three periods are linked by descriptions of two transitional periods, one under the Judges (46:1-12) and the other under leaders of the restoration (49:11-13).

One noteworthy feature of the Praise of the Wise Ancestors is the prominent place given to worship and to the high priests Aaron and Simon (45:6-22 and 50:1-21). R. Hayward suggests the reason is the analogy between the descriptions of Simon and wisdom (cf. 50:9-12

125

and 24:13-15). Simon makes present in the liturgy the action of Wisdom herself, the order willed by God and always offered to human beings. Thus, the liturgical acts of Simon take on cosmic proportions, especially since the liturgy takes place on Mount Zion, the point of divine presence in the world. Since Aaron's task was "to enlighten Israel with his law" (45:17), and authentic wisdom implied observing the commandments, worship furthered the rule of wisdom.[12]

THE MAIN TEACHINGS OF SIRACH

Since Sirach is a vast anthology, almost twice as long as Proverbs, enormous effort is required to understand the book well. The preceding section, "Key Passages," provided one approach, the study of key *texts* in the book. This section provides another approach, the study of important *topics* in the book. Listed here are the chief topics of Sirach and the passages where they are best represented, along with some introductory remarks. Sirach, more than any other biblical wisdom writer, has a "doctrine."

Wisdom and the Sage

The primary role of wisdom in the book is shown by its presence in the key passages in the book. Every one of the eight parts of the book is prefaced by a poem on wisdom (recall Skehan and Di Lella's outline). The opening poem (1:1-10) states that wisdom is with God, is inaccessible to human beings, and is given to those whom God loves. The next poem, verses 11-30, is concerned with relating wisdom to the great virtue in Sirach, fear of the Lord (see the discussion that follows). Chapter 4:11-19 personifies wisdom as a mother educating her children, who does not shield them from painful but necessary trials. In 6:18-37, Ben Sira makes use of three analogies to show the virtues needed in acquiring wisdom: the patience of a farmer (vv. 18-22), the endurance of a prisoner combined with the endurance of a hunter (vv. 23-31), and willingness to associate with those who are wise (vv. 32-37). Chapters 14:20–15:10 personify wisdom as a wife and mother in order to show her benefits to those who seek her. Chapter 24 is the central poem on wisdom, and has been examined under "Key Passages." The poem personifies wisdom and identifies her with the word of God (24:3) and hence with the Law (24:3).

Chapter 24 says something important about the vocation of the sage. It compares Wisdom to the great cosmic rivers that fertilize the earth, allowing the sage to define himself as one who draws from that world-encompassing stream (vv. 30-34).

> As for me, I was like a canal from a river,
>   like a water channel into a garden.
> I said, "I will water my garden
>   and drench my flower-beds."
> And lo, my canal became a river,
>   and my river a sea.
> I will again make instruction shine forth like the dawn,
>   and I will make it clear from far away.
> I will again pour out teaching like prophecy,
>   and leave it to all future generations.
> Observe that I have not labored for myself alone,
>   but for all who seek wisdom.[13]

The sage compares himself to a rivulet from that mighty river, which first fertilizes his own garden and then, without his seeming to take a further step, increases and becomes fruitful for others ("And lo, my canal became a river"). The sage's words do not simply represent his own wisdom but are God's words to future generations, like prophecy. Further relevant texts on the vocation of the scribe include 37:16-26, which champions the discernment one expects to see in a true scribe, and 39:1-11, which idealizes the scribe as a keen student of Scripture, an advisor to the great, a traveler to foreign lands, a hard worker, and devout servant of God who realizes that all knowledge comes from God. Ben Sira ends with autobiographical verses on his love of wisdom, how he has pursued her from youth.

Fear of the Lord

"Fear of the Lord" was a venerable concept in the ancient Near East long before Sirach. It was part of a self-understanding by which one realized one's place in a world the gods had made exclusively for themselves, which led one to revere and recognize their dominion. Ben Sira highlighted this virtue beyond others to a point that some commentators see it as the dominant virtue in the book.[14]

Others concede its importance, but still argue for the primacy of wisdom in Sirach as in other wisdom books.[15] Fear of the Lord, or revering Yahweh, is the basic attitude of those who would acquire wisdom. In the book, fear of the Lord is not, however, subordinate to wisdom, playing merely an instrumental role in its acquisition. The moral life begins and ends in fear of the Lord, which synthesizes human beings' relationship to God. The three concepts of wisdom, fear of the Lord, and the law, are intimately related in Sirach, and in some texts they appear almost to be equivalent, but that is an impression derived from the associative logic of Ben Sira.

The poem in 1:11-30, examined in detail under "Key Passages," is the most explicit text on the relationship of the two concepts. The poem declares that fear of the Lord is the beginning and completion, the crown and the root of wisdom (1:14-20). It seems to be the human attitude that one needs so that wisdom can be given as a gift.

The Law

By way of preface to the topic of law, everyone should recognize that the equation of law and legalism in this period is an outdated stereotype of Second Temple Judaism. As expected of a sage writing in the wisdom tradition, Ben Sira rarely invokes the Law as a motive for conduct. He teaches the honoring of parents in 3:1-16 without mentioning the Decalogue. He does, however, mention the Law a few times, when he speaks about the duty to give the priest his due (7:31), about forgoing anger against the neighbor (28:7), about aiding the poor (29:9), about not appearing before the Lord empty-handed (35:6-7), and about a woman caught in adultery (23:23).

Ben Sira uses law in two senses. The first is law as a general reference to the commandments. In this sense, law, fear of the Lord, and wisdom are closely related terms, at times virtually identical. The second is law as Torah in the sense of 24:23, "All this (= wisdom) is the covenant of the Most High God, / the law that Moses commanded us." Law designates the whole revelation in the Bible; in this sense law is the wisdom always offered to human beings.

Prayer

Ben Sira speaks of prayer more than any sage. The book itself has three lengthy prayers, 22:27–23:6, a petition for control of one's words and of the sexual instinct; 36:1-22, a supplication for the deliverance of Zion; and 51:1-12, a psalm of thanksgiving. His teaching on prayer runs through the book. Of the genres of prayers, petition is the most recommended. He urges prayer for forgiveness (21:1; 28:2-4; 34:30-31; 39:5), for wise counsel (37:15), for healing (38:9, 13-14), for wisdom (51:13-14). He uses heroes of the past as examples of petitioners before God, Joshua (46:5), Samuel (46:16), and Hezekiah (48:20). He also urges praise of God (17:10-9 [*sic*]; 39:14-15, 35; 43:30). As to conduct during prayer, he tells people not to babble on (7:10) and not to be discouraged (7:14). Obey the commandments if you want your prayer to be heard (3:5), for prayer and sin are incompatible (34:30-31; 15:9).

Nature and History

The traditional realm of wisdom literature was personal and familial. It was not concerned with national history, but Ben Sira extended the range of wisdom's purview. He envisioned wisdom more broadly than any of his predecessors. It is clear from chapter 24 and 42:15–50:24 that wisdom is God's word that created the world and guided human history, especially Israelite history. Wisdom is not given only to individuals for their personal and familial lives. It also operates in the natural world and in the course of history. Earlier sages drew their arguments almost exclusively from personal conduct and the interaction of God and individuals and, occasionally, from the near-human conduct of animals such as ants and leeches (cf. Prov 6:6-9; 30:24-31). Ben Sira, traditional sage that he is, draws much of his argument from this sphere, but he now includes (1) the history of Israel and (2) the beautiful and smoothly running *universe*. With regard to (1), "history" for Ben Sira is an appropriate topic for a sage, but he sees it as a series of wisdom-inspired individuals, Adam (49:16) and Noah (44:17-18), and especially Israelites—the ancestor Abraham, Moses, the priest Aaron, David, Elijah, Josiah, and the priest Simon. Some individuals rejected the wisdom given to them to govern Israel, such as Solomon's son Rehoboam, "broad in folly and lacking in sense" (47:23) and most of the kings, who "abandoned the law of the Most High" (49:4; cf. 24:23).[16] He retells the canonical outline (as was common in the literature of the time) but gives his particular slant. With regard to the regularity of the universe (2), Ben Sira is possibly influenced by the Stoic doctrine of the Logos immanent in the world and its championing of a "natural law" to which the human race ought to conform. The created world's regularity or "obedience" can be a model for human beings: "When the Lord created his works from the beginning . . . he arranged his works in an eternal order. . . . They neither hunger nor grow weary . . . and they never disobey his word" (16:26-28). The universe does not, however, work to a noble purpose without exception. "All the works of the Lord are good" (39:33), to be sure, but God's works come forth in pairs (33:14-15; 39:27; 42:24-25) and the destiny of each is different. The destiny of some comes to fulfillment, but of others, to punishment.

Divine Sovereignty and Human Freedom

Though the Bible customarily affirms divine sovereignty *and* human freedom without seeing contradiction or exploring the "problem," Ben Sira does feel an obligation to reassert human freedom and responsibility. He is forced to do so because some denied it: "Do not say, 'It was the Lord's doing that I fell away'; . . . 'It was he who led me astray' " (15:11-12); "Do not say, 'I am hidden from the Lord, and who from on high has me in mind?' " (16:17). Ben Sira does not, as we have seen under "Key Passages" (15:11-20), use the rabbinic doctrine of the "evil instinct." He argues for human freedom on the basis of the nature of human beings (cf. "if you choose" in 15:15) and the character of God (15:11-20). He gives a rational foundation for human freedom by invoking the traditional doctrine on the "two ways" and by his own doctrine of opposites or pairs (33:7-15). A recent study by G. Prato concludes that Ben Sira finds a solution in his understanding of creation:

Creation is seen as a harmonious arrangement of realities coming forth in pairs (33:7-15). According to how they are used, these realities are capable of receiving a different destiny and can thus be changed equally into an instrument of punishment (39:16-35). On the human plane, this means that human beings are substantially free; if they are punished, it can be put down to their abusing their freedom. If one examines the original intent of creation, all fatalism is excluded (15:11–17:14). In formulating his doctrine, Ben Sira is acutely aware of the limits of human language on the issue. That awareness shows up in a positive way when he presents the variety of creation under the form of a list and then passes immediately to celebrating the praise of wisdom (42:15–43:33). The awareness appears in a negative way when he acknowledges the bitter aspects of existence (suffering and death, 40:1-17; 41:1-13).[17]

130

Life in Society

As already noted, Ben Sira insists on the primacy of wisdom and its active presence in both nature and history (including the Law), and on revering the Lord as the human disposition that clears the ground for the divine gift of wisdom. Many of the details of his moral teaching are traditional: mastery of self especially of one's tongue (19:4-17; 20:5-8; 23:12-15; 27:4-6; and so forth) and fulfillment of duties. One interesting topic is his insistence that people retain proper esteem of themselves and enjoy themselves: "My child, honor yourself with humility, / and give yourself the esteem you deserve" (10:28); "My child, treat yourself well, according to your means, / and present worthy offerings to the Lord"; "Do not deprive yourself of a day's enjoyment; / do not let your share of desired good pass by you" (14:11, 14).

Ben Sira was traditional in his teachings about the family. The father's authority over the house was absolute, and he only addressed young men. He imposes on them, however, the duty of caring for aged parents (3:1-6). His teachings on women are exceptionally severe. He admires harmony between married couples (25:1) and understands the importance to a man of a good wife (26:1-4; 36:26-31). On the other hand, he is unusually sensitive to temptations coming from "the strange woman" (forbidden) and from a prostitute (9:1-9; 26:9-12; 42:12-14).[18]

RECOMMENDED READING

Commentaries

Crenshaw, James L. "The Book of Sirach," in *The New Interpreter's Bible*, vol. 5. Nashville: Abingdon Press, 1997. Pp. 601-867. Erudite, up-to-date, with a theological perspective.

Kearns, C. "Ecclesiasticus," in B. Orchard, ed., *A New Catholic Commentary on Sacred Scripture*. London: Nelson, 1969.

Skehan, Patrick W., Alexander A. Di Lella. *The Wisdom of Ben Sira*. Anchor Bible 39. New York: Doubleday, 1989. The standard in English, with special attention to the thorny problem of the texts.

Snaith, J. G. *Ecclesiasticus*. Cambridge Bible Commentary. Cambridge: Cambridge University, 1974.

Studies

Collins, John J. *Jewish Wisdom in the Hellenistic Age* Old Testament Library. Louisville: Westminster John Knox, 1997. Pp. 21-131. Excellent discussion of the theological ideas.

Crenshaw, James L. "The Problem of Theodicy in Sirach: On Human Bondage." *JBL* 94 (1975): 46-64.

Di Lella, Alexander A. "The Meaning of Wisdom in Ben Sira," in Leo Perdue, ed. *In Search of Wisdom: Essays in Memory of John G. Gammie.* Louisville, Ky.: Westminster, 1993. Pp. 133-48.

Sanders, Jack T. *Ben Sira and Demotic Wisdom.* SBLMS 28. Chico, Calif.: Scholars Press, 1983.

CHAPTER 7

THE WISDOM OF
SOLOMON

The Wisdom of Solomon, also called the Book of Wisdom, is, like The Wisdom of Ben Sira (Sirach), one of the Apocrypha or Deuterocanonical books, which are not considered canonical by Protestants or Jews but are so reckoned by Roman Catholics and Orthodox.

At first reading the Wisdom of Solomon seems to address a different world from that of the wisdom books we have examined so far. It threatens kings and commands them to obey ("Listen therefore, O kings, and understand / learn, O judges of the ends of the earth," 6:1), speaks of the resurrection of the dead ("Then the righteous will stand with great confidence / in the presence of those who have oppressed them," 5:1), and talks about the end of the present world and a future judgment (4:16–5:23). The book also contains obvious references to the history of Israel, though without naming names: Solomon is to be understood as the wise king in chapters 7–9; the seven portraits of Genesis characters who were guided by wisdom in chapter 10, though not named, are easily identified as Adam, Cain (and Abel), Noah, Abraham, Lot, Jacob, Joseph; with the disguised allusion to Moses in 10:15–11:14 there begins a retelling of the exodus story that will only end in 19:22. More than half the book uses the history of Israel or prominent Israelites to illustrate God's wise governance of the world. Wisdom of Solomon goes beyond Sirach's praise of famous Israelites in chapters 44–50, for the history of Israel is intrinsic to its argument in a way that it is not for Sirach.

Despite its unique features, however, Wisdom of Solomon is indisputably an Israelite wisdom book. As in the other books, Solomon is the wise king, an example and mediator of wisdom. As Proverbs described human behavior in terms of pairs—the righteous and wicked persons or the lazy and diligent persons—so Wisdom of Solomon employs types, the violent and the righteous (or wise) individuals. It poses choices in the stark vocabulary of life and death and employs the metaphor of the two ways. A characteristic feature of biblical wisdom literature is the quest for the order in the universe, an order that is not obvious and requires constant seeking. That hidden order (or world) is also an important theme of Wisdom of Solomon. Measured by its themes and concerns, therefore, Wisdom of Solomon belongs securely to the corpus of biblical wisdom books.

HISTORICAL BACKGROUND

Why is Wisdom of Solomon so different from older wisdom books and yet so similar in its themes? One reason for any book's distinctiveness, of course, is its author, but we know nothing about the author. Another reason is its social context, and we know something about that. Wisdom of Solomon was composed in Greek probably in the Egyptian city of Alexandria, most likely in the first century B.C.E. It is the only wisdom book that originated in Hellenistic Judaism rather than Palestinian Judaism.

What do we know about Jews in Egypt? The histories and cultures of Egypt and Palestine were associated from time immemorial. Egypt was the dominant power in Palestine in the second millennium, ruling its province of Canaan (the southern part of the Levant) through local princes and strategically placed garrisons. In the first millennium Egypt was often allied with Israel (as a somewhat inconstant partner) against Aramaic city-states (ninth century), the Neo-Assyrian Empire (eighth to seventh centuries), and the Neo-Babylonian Empire (late-seventh to sixth centuries). During the period of the Persian Empire (539–333 B.C.E.), both Palestine and Egypt were subject states. In 333 B.C.E. Alexander the Great defeated Persia and swept through the Near East. After Alexander's death in 323 B.C.E., his vast empire was divided among his generals, among whom were Ptolemy I (323–285 B.C.E.) and Seleucus I (312–280 B.C.E.). Palestine was under the Ptolemies until 198 B.C.E. (Battle of Panium), after which the Seleucids exercised control. Seleucid control yielded to native rule in 163 B.C.E., the Hasmonean dynasty. In 63 B.C.E., the powerful Roman Empire entered the area. Thereafter the Hasmonean dynasty, and from 37 B.C.E., the Herodian dynasty, ruled under Rome's supervision.

Though Israel had relationships with other countries and empires, Egypt was special because of its proximity and place in biblical tradition. In the stories of the ancestors Egypt was a place of wealth and plentiful grain, a refuge for those in uncertain agricultural climates. It could also be dangerous, as the Hebrews learned through bitter experience. Genesis and Exodus tell how the large family of Jacob at first found relief from famine and then just as suddenly became slaves. In the religious imagination of Israel Egypt was remembered as a place of strange customs, grandeur, and slavery. Despite its role in the literature as oppressive, Egypt was also a place of refuge. Solomon's enemy Hadad fled to Egypt (1 Kgs 11:14-22), and in the sixth-century Exile many Israelites fled to Egypt. By the fifth century there was a Jewish settlement, including a temple, at Elephantine on the southern border of Egypt. From ca. 173 B.C.E. to 71 C.E. there was another Jewish temple at Leontopolis in the eastern delta.

The capital of Ptolemaic Egypt and the main Mediterranean port was Alexandria, founded by Alexander the Great in 331 B.C.E. It was one of the largest and grandest cities in the world, famous for the tomb of Alexander, its museum and library (400,000 volumes), and great lighthouse. Theoretically, it was an autonomous *polis* (city). Its citizens came from all over the Greek world, though there were other ethnic groups, including a large Jewish community, that had acquired special privileges though not citizenship. The dynastic struggles of the later Ptolemies affected the city, and the turmoil exacerbated the long-standing antagonism between the "Greek" citizen-body and the local Jewish community.

Alexandria was a port city in more than one sense. Goods from all over the Mediterranean passed through its docks, and so did new ideas. Ancient Greek texts were copied and commented upon in its great library. The Jewish community was also active intellectually, engaging its own religious traditions and contemporary intellectual currents. Beginning in the third century B.C.E. and lasting well into the next century, scholars began translating the Hebrew Scriptures into Greek, to serve the needs of a whole generation of Jews who had grown up unable to read their scriptures in Hebrew. The translation, without precedent in the ancient world in its scope and method, is called the Septuagint according to a legend that seventy-two translators were involved.[1] The Jews of Alexandria were open to contemporary thinking, to judge by Philo, a wealthy statesman and philosopher (ca. 20 B.C.E.–50 C.E.) who combined a loyalty toward his own Judaism with a love for Greek philosophy. Using the allegorical method current in interpreting ancient texts, he sought to make Jewish thought compatible with Stoic, Pythagorean, and especially Middle Platonic ideas. Other authors also put the ancient traditions in a new context—3 Maccabees and perhaps 2 and 4 Maccabees, and Wisdom of Solomon.

HELLENISTIC JUDAISM

Alexander the Great (356–323 B.C.E.) initiated a great cultural movement, which has left its effect on Wisdom of Solomon—Hellenistic culture.[2] "Hellenistic" is an adjective for Greek culture ("Hellenism") in its interaction with the native cultures of the East. The age was the first great marketplace of ideas. The old cultures and societies of the ancient East, ruled by tradition and custom, were confronted by new ideas, procedures, and people. Two relevant areas can be singled out, religion and philosophy. Enthusiastic advocates, or preachers, of the new religions traveled from city to city expounding their views and looking for followers. The various religions and philosophies were not regarded solely as doctrines but as ways of life. Each doctrine had implications for living. Hellenistic religions and philosophies were intellectual-ethical systems.

Hellenistic religion had certain emphases, three of which left their mark on Wisdom of Solomon. The first was miracles. Performing miracles was what made a god. Lists of a god's miracles constituted a distinct literary genre—an aretalogy. Certain miracles were particularly impressive: cures of blindness, especially blindness from birth; rescues from disasters at sea such as sending up fresh water through the brine; transformations or metamorphoses, for example, turning a man-turned-into-an-animal back into a man. Another feature of Hellenistic religion was its interest in immortality. Immortality was a gift of the gods. In pre-Hellenistic Judaism, this life was the only life. But in the Hellenistic marketplace of ideas, a successful religion had to offer immortality. Even in Egypt, where life after death had always been offered, it was offered to more people than before. A third feature was the claim of great antiquity. A religion had to be old, for what was new needed validation by the old. Three ancient events were often cited as standards of antiquity: (1) Semiramis, the legendary founder of Assyria; (2) the Trojan War, the oldest datable event in Greek history; and (3) the Flood.

All these emphases appear in Wisdom of Solomon. Wisdom 11–19 portrays the Exodus as a series of miracles in which natural elements change their properties; immortality is one of the chief topics, a striking difference from earlier books; the first person guided by wisdom was Adam, "the first-formed father of the world, when he alone had been created" (10:1); the cast of characters includes Noah "when the earth was flooded" (10:4-5). Even more important than the individual points is the fact that the author of Wisdom has entered the competition. He wants to persuade fellow Jews of the contemporary relevance of the Jewish faith in the midst of rival claims.

A word must be said about Hellenistic philosophy relevant to Wisdom. The dominant philosophies were Stoicism and Middle Platonism. In essence, the Stoics held that God was the immanent principle of energy by which the natural world is created and sustained. He is also the world reason or Logos manifesting itself in the beauty and order of the world. The ideal human beings were the wise, conforming themselves to nature, living according to the law of the universe.

Middle Platonism (ca. 80 B.C.E.–250 C.E.) in ethics held that rational activity should aim at the *summum bonum* or "end of goods." Some circles formulated this as "likeness to God." Other issues were the relation of God's providence to human free will; the question whether creation was an eternal process or a single act; and the hierarchy of being.

Popularized aspects of Stoicism, Middle Platonism, and indeed of other philosophies are found in Wisdom of Solomon, especially in chapters 13–15. Examples of general Greek influence are the four virtues (the Christian "cardinal" virtues), temperance, prudence, justice, and fortitude (8:7), and the reckoning of fire, wind, air, or stars as an animating force in the world (13:2). Examples of Stoic influence are the world soul (7:24), the proof from design (13:1), and the typically Stoic mode of argument, the sorites (chain argument) in 8:17-21. Derived from Platonism are the preexistence of the soul (8:19), the sharp distinction between body and soul (8:20; 9:15), and the lesser reality of the material world compared with the spiritual world of heaven (9:15-16).

THE STRUCTURE OF THE BOOK

For other wisdom books, the best starting point is the genre. If one knows the genre, one knows what to expect. With Wisdom of Solomon, however, the approach from genre is not so helpful, for the genre is disputed—is it epideictic (praise) as practiced in Greek and Latin rhetoric, or protreptic? Neither is familiar to modern readers. We begin, then, with a literary analysis of the book.[3]

Ancient works were not written with headings and paragraph divisions to guide the reader. Ancient works, no less rational and artful than modern works, relied on internal hints and directions that would have been easily caught by an experienced reader. Two of the most common hints are repetitions of words, usually at the beginning and end of sections (= *inclusio*), and *chiasm*, also called envelope or sandwich construction, in which an idea is developed with an ABCDC′B′A′ pattern. Such structuring clues are used in Wisdom of Solomon, which is, even by ancient standards, a complex and dense work.

Given its complexity and cross-referencing, we approach it initially by means of the following schematic outline, in three parts.[4] The outline makes visible the chiasms and, by means of brief notes, informs the reader of the main points. Comment on the coherence of the whole follows the outline. Following that is comment on Wisdom's principal themes—justice and immortality, wisdom's governance of the world, Israel as the chosen people, and how to attain wisdom.

138

THE WISDOM OF SOLOMON

The Outline

PART I (1:1–6:21): The Two Worlds

A Exhortation: God reveals himself, Wisdom is hidden; seek her!
      (1:1-12)   legal judgment
  B Plan of the impious: introduction—creation,
          (1:13–2:24) judgment of the author
               speech—meaning of life, way of life
                  —assault on the just person
               conclusion—judgment of the author,
                    creation incorruptible
    C Diptychs: death of the just, impious
        (3–4)   virtue without children,
                 children of adulterers (twice)
  B' Confession of the impious: introduction—just, impious
       (5:1-23)   speech—triumph of the just
               —way of life, meaning of life
               conclusion—impious, just
                    God and the final cosmic combat
A' Exhortation: legal judgment
  (6:1-21) Wisdom reveals herself; seek her! incorruptibility

PART II (6:22–10:21): Wisdom and the Way to It

6:22–8:21 is composed of seven passages in concentric order.
6:22-25 introduces the themes.
A The origin of Solomon is like any human being's (7:1-6, vv. 1 and
  6 "the same for all")
  B So I prayed for wisdom (7:7-12)
    C communication of knowledge of God to Solomon (7:13-22*a*,
      vv. 13*b* and 21*a*; Greek root *krupt-*, "hide" and "secret" in NRSV)
      D Praise of wisdom, its nature, origin, action (v. 21); attri-
        butes (7:22*b*–8:1)
    C' Solomon will marry wisdom, who lives with God (8:2-9)
  B' thoughts of the young Solomon (8:10-16)
A' young Solomon will ask for wisdom (8:17-21, vv. 17*b*, 21*d* "heart")

Chap. 9: Prayer of Solomon. Chapters 7 and 8 point toward the
prayer at their beginning (7:7) and end (8:21). The prayer itself is
in three parts, verses 1-6 human being, 7-12 "Solomon," 13-18 human being. It is the center of the book in that the beginning of the
prayer is about creation (theme of Part I), and its end is about salvation ("saved" in v. 18 = theme of Part II).

Chap. 10: Enumeration of heroes. Eight episodes of prominent heroes of Genesis, all contrasted with an opposition they encountered. Abel is implicitly opposed to his brother Cain. All except Cain are beneficiaries of wisdom; she comes to their rescue. Reference to prayer in 10:20 is inclusio of 19:9 at end of the book.

PART III (11:1–19:22): The Exodus

Seven Comparisons (Greek *synkrisis*) from Exodus (11:1-14 + 16:1–19:22)

Comparison 1. 11:6-14 *flowing water*—water from the rock[5]
Two excursus or digressions (11:15–15:19), one on the moderation of God toward those whom he punishes (Egypt and Canaan; 11:15–12:27), the second a critique of the gods (13–15). The excursus are linked to the main theme by 11:15; 12:23-27; and 15:18-19.

Excursus 1. Moderation of God toward Egypt and Canaan (11:15–12:27)

Excursus 2. Critique of worshipers (13:1–15:19)
   1. 13:1-9 ("foolish" 13:1) philosophers, especially the Stoic
   2. 13:10–15:13 ("miserable" 13:10) image venerators
      a 13:10-19 idols, role of woodcutter
        b 14:1-10 invocation of God, reference to history
          c 14:11-31 chastisement
        b′ 15:1-6 invocation of God, reference to history
      a′ 15:7-13 idols, role of potter
   3. 15:14-19 ("most foolish" 15:14) Egyptians, venerators of idols and animals, oppressors of holy people

Comparison 2. 16:1-4 *frogs*—quails
Comparison 3. 16:5-14 *flies and locusts*—bronze serpent
Comparison 4. 16:15-29 *storm and hail*—manna
Comparison 5. 17:1–18:4 *darkness*—light
Comparison 6. 18:5-25 *Death of firstborn*—Israel spared
Comparison 7. 19:1-9 *drowning in the Red Sea*—passage
           19:10-22 is a summary of chief episodes in the diptychs and final critique of the impious; last verse broadens the perspective: God glorifies his people everywhere and always.

Analysis of the outline. We begin with Part I, 1:1–6:21, which is recognized as a unit within the book by its chiastic structure. The outline makes clear the main cross-references. A is echoed and reprised by A', B by B', C by C', and D stands alone as the center. An ancient reader would realize that A' (6:1-21) refers back to A (1:1-12) and brings its themes to completion, that is, legal judgment (of kings) and wisdom coming forth from her hiddenness. In B (1:13–2:24), the impious reveal their nihilistic philosophy of life and their contempt for the just person, but in B' (5:1-23) they retract their statements and admit they were wrong. In C, the diptychs (matching sketches) contrast the just and the impious in important areas. There are further logical devices, of which only a few can be pointed out: 1:13-15 points back to verse 1 by "righteousness" and "earth" but (much more important) points forward to chapter 2: "because God" in 1:13 is reprised in 2:23; "make" or "create" occurs in 1:13-14 and 2:23; "world" *(kosmos)* occurs in 1:14 and 2:24; "death" occurs in 1:12, 13 and 2:20, 24. What is the meaning of this ancient form of "paragraphing"? Structurally, it informs the reader that 1:13–2:24 form a logical section; as one reads 2:23-24, one will hear echoes of 1:13–2:1 and conclude that the section is ending. Semantically, the opening affirmation that God's world is coherent and generative (1:13-15) is contradicted by the speech of the impious (1:16–2:20), setting up a dramatic tension between divine purpose and human intent. Thus are established the basic antitheses of chapters 1–6, death and life, the just person and the impious, God and human rulers.

We can more briefly analyze Parts II and III. Part II, like Part I, has a chiasm in chapters 7–8, introduced by 6:22-25. The "kings" in Part I have changed to *the* king, Solomon (not named in accord with the typifying tendency of wisdom literature). The theme is now wisdom, its nature, origin, and action (the center of the chiasm, 7:22b–8:1), and how wisdom works in Solomon. The whole section is oriented toward the prayer of Solomon, who is the great exemplar of wisdom. Chapter 10 is a list of "wisdom heroes" in Genesis, comparable to Sirach 44–49 and Hebrews 11. At the end of chapter 10, the reference to praising God is an inclusio to be reprised at the end of the book (19:9).

Part III, 11:1–19:22, is linked to the previous part by Moses the eighth (unnamed) wisdom hero in 11:1. With Moses, the theme changes to the exodus, which is depicted as seven miracles or transformations of natural phenomena in favor of the just (the Israelites). There are two excursus, one short and one long, which are inserted into the text rather than placed at its end.

141

GENRE

Like other works of Greek literature, especially from the third century B.C.E. forward, Wisdom was composed with a knowledge of classical rhetorical theory. In his *On Rhetoric,* Aristotle distinguished three categories of rhetoric, which remained fundamental throughout the history of classical rhetoric: judicial, in which the audience is asked to make a decision about the past, deliberative, in which the audience is asked to make a decision about the future, and epideictic (= "demonstrative"), which does not require a decision from the audience. Examples of the last are speeches given at ceremonial occasions, or those aimed at giving praise or blame. Wisdom of Solomon fits within this last category. The book praises a way of life—the way of wisdom—and invites others to search for it. Some scholars seek to be more precise in naming the genre. J. Reese suggests the book falls within a subcategory of epideictic rhetoric—protreptic, which is an exhortation (to philosophy). It was first developed as a genre by the fifth-century sophists, who used it to persuade students to take their courses in philosophy and other arts.[6] No early examples of the genre are extant. M. Gilbert prefers the genre *encomium* or "praise" of a person or entity, in which case the exordium is Wisdom 1:1–6:21, the praise, 6:22–9:18, the *synkrisis* (comparison) drawn from the past, chapters 10–19, and the epilogue, 19:22.[7]

Though the genre provides only a general framework, in this case it gives an important clue about the purpose of Wisdom of Solomon. The protreptic, or praise, is designed not for the forum or law court but for the marketplace of ideas in a Hellenistic city. Hellenistic religions and philosophies (which often saw themselves as ways of life) competed for new disciples, and needed to advertise themselves by boasting of miracles, immortality, and great antiquity. Wisdom of Solomon is marked by that same competitiveness. It addresses the young, the searching, and those discontent with the limits of their own philosophy or religion. In comparison with these new ways of life, traditional Judaism might look old-fashioned and rigid, a thing of the past. The author makes an elaborate case for the ancient faith, portraying it as an attractive and vital choice.

THE BOOK: AN ANALYSIS OF ITS THREE PARTS

With the tripartite structure of Wisdom of Solomon as our point of reference, what follows is an analysis of each part in turn, followed at the end by a synthesis of the entire book.

Part I (1:1–6:21): The Two Worlds

This section provides a theory underlying an ethics, as did Hellenistic philosophies. "Two worlds" is an apt title for the entire section, for it contrasts the transitory world of appearances ruled over by the devil, destined to pass away, which has its own citizens, the impious (1:16; 2:23; 5:6, 13-14; and so forth), and the true world created by God, destined to be immortal, which has its own citizens, the righteous (1:14-15; 3:7-9; 4:13-16). The transitory world is the world of our daily experience. The true world is not visible in the same way. It comes to visibility when people choose wisdom, that is, undergo trustingly the persecution of the righteous that leads to their exaltation and public vindication. The righteous person's drama of humiliation and exaltation is the instrument by which the true world is revealed.[8] That, in brief, is the essence of chapters 1–6. Let us look at the units.

In A of the chiasm (see our outline) the book addresses kings (1:1; 6:1), whom it regards as regents of the one God whether they know it or not, like the Assyrian king in Isaiah 10:5-19, the Babylonian king in Jeremiah 29:10, and the Persian king in Isaiah 45:1-7. Kings of the time would ordinarily be thought of as wise and powerful, but if they are unaware of the true ruler, they risk judgment and punishment. In 1:1-12, "righteousness," "goodness," "wisdom," and "spirit of the Lord" are near synonyms. Thus the first twelve verses deny the absolute authority of human kings, and condemn it if it is not under wisdom. One should also read "A'" in the outline (6:1-21) as another statement of the same point.

In B of the great chiasm, the adherents of the world of appearances (the wicked) express their core views in a lengthy speech (2:1-20). As noted in the outline, 1:13-15 is the transition between A and B and also points ahead to the end of B. Words in 1:13-15 appear again at the end, subtly informing the reader that the unit is complete: "because God" appears in 1:13 and 2:23; "to make" or "create" and "world" in 1:13-14 and 2:24; "death" in 1:12, 13 and 2:20, 24.

How does the author present the speech of the ungodly? Their speech (2:1-20) is framed by "bookend" comments in 1:13-16 and 2:21-24. The first bookend affirms that God made the world wholesome and did not make death; righteousness is immortal (*athanatos*). The ungodly invited death and belong to his company (*meris*, 1:16; 2:9, 24). The other bookend at the end of chapter 2 echoes the positive judgment of creation. How differently the ungodly see things! There is no purpose in life, all is chance, and death is the end ("no return from death" in vv. 1 and 5). Let us give ourselves to pleasure, live for the moment (vv. 6-9), let us attack the righteous person (vv. 10-20). The bookend (2:21-24) judges their reasoning to be erroneous, for they do not recognize the "mysteries of God," which are God's plans for the world.[9] The ungodly do not, in short, recognize the true nature of the world as it is described at the opening of the book (1:1-12 + 13-16): there is a divine spirit (or wisdom or justice) in the world holding it together (1:7); this wisdom is invisible to the ungodly "party" yet it will judge them; this hidden world is immortal (1:12-16).

Chapters 1-2 combine aspects of Middle Platonism and biblical wisdom. The hidden order of the world is compatible with Platonic tradition, with its clear distinction between two levels of reality, the intelligible world (God, the Ideas, the contents of the divine mind, which are copied by things of the world) and the world perceived by the senses. At the same time, the view of two worlds in Wisdom of Solomon is a transposition of the hidden wisdom in earlier biblical wisdom literature. Proverbs urges its readers to seek wisdom above all things, characterizing it as hidden and graspable only by the virtuous; the wicked do not see it and will be punished by it. In addition, the wisdom literature developed the doctrine of the two ways: before every person two ways lie, each with its allotted fate (cf. Prov 4:10-19).

If the "ontology" of the chapters is traditional, immortality as a quality of human beings is new in a biblical book. In the earlier sections of the Bible the only kind of human life is lived in this world and ends with death, except for a shadowy existence in Sheol. Resurrection of the body is first mentioned in Daniel 12:1-3, about 164 B.C.E., in connection with the death of heroically loyal Jews and the fate of their killers: "Many of those who sleep in the dust of the earth shall awake, some to everlasting life, and some to shame and everlasting contempt." But this resurrection is not immortality. Immortality of the soul is of Greek origin (deduced by them from the kinship of the soul with the eternal principles of reason). Wisdom of Solomon adds its biblical perspective to the Greek view. Unlike the Platonic tradition, immortality is not innate but granted by God as a gift to those who seek wisdom or pursue righteousness.

The individual who demonstrates the falseness of the world of appearances and makes the real world visible is the righteous trusting person, the "child of the Lord" (2:13). He provokes the wicked to make a test: "Let us condemn him to a shameful death, for according to what he says, he will be protected." The just person is therefore the instrument by which the true world becomes visible. More precisely, it is through the death of the righteous person at the hands of the ungodly that God will be revealed as God, but the full import of this statement will only become clear in chapters 3–5.

The middle unit of Part I is chapters 3–4, C in the chiasm. The unit contains a series of diptychs, which contrast the just (3:1-9) and the ungodly (3:10-12), their spouses and children. Verse 12 sounds the theme: "Their wives are foolish, and their children evil; / their offspring are accursed." Traditionally in the Bible, "immortality" was surviving after death in one's name and one's children. The little sketches show righteous individuals without children "having fruit" and having a place in the temple of the Lord (3:13-15), whereas children of adulterers do not attain maturity (3:16-19). Chapter 4:10-15 cites, without using his name, biblical Enoch (Gen 5:21-24), as an example of someone who was "taken up" to heaven at a younger age than the other pre-Flood heroes so as not to be defiled.[10] In his case, his early "removal" preserved him from defilement. Chapter 5 is B' of the chiasm. It contains the speech of the ungodly (vv. 4-13) in which they retract point-by-point their first speech in 2:1-20: they admit it was they, not the just person, who were wrong and misunderstood the nature of the universe (as it was described in 1:1-12). Several words link chapter 5 to chapter 2, particularly "the just man" in 5:1 and 2:12, and "son of God" in 5:5 and 2:18.

Two important ideas need to be pointed out, one expressed in the opening verses, 5:1-5, and the other in the closing verses, 5:15-23. Verses 1-5 make clear that it is the sight of the just person, whom the ungodly killed but is now rescued by God, that enables the ungodly to confess their error: "Why have they been numbered among the children of God? / And why is their lot among the saints?" The just person has been elevated to the heavenly world to join the angels, a conception found in Daniel 12:2-3, *1 Enoch* 104:2, 6; and 1QH 3:19-23. The death and resurrection of the just person is the means by which the true world becomes visible. A second important idea is in verses 17-23: "Creation will join with [the Lord] to fight against his frenzied foes" (v. 20b). The idea is a restatement of 1:14, "for [God] created all things so that they might exist, / the generative forces of the world are wholesome, / and there is no destructive poison in them, / and the dominion of Hades is not on earth." The world, spiritual and physical, is under God and itself punishes wrongdoers; the world is self-righting, for it is made by the righteous God.[11]

Wisdom of Solomon expounds an important biblical theme in chapter 5, the exaltation and vindication of the just person. The theme is found in the story of Joseph in Genesis 37-50, Ahiqar, Esther, Daniel 3 and 6, Susanna. In the early form of the story, the protagonist is a wise man in a royal court. Maliciously accused of a crime, he is condemned to death, but then vindicated of the charge and exalted to a high rank, and his enemies are punished. Wisdom of Solomon makes three changes in the traditional form: (1) the exaltation scene in chapter 5 is expanded by borrowing from the suffering servant passage in Isaiah 52:13–53:12; (2) the protagonist is actually put to death; (3) the just person is exalted to the heavenly court where he serves as vice-regent of the heavenly king. The new doctrine of immortality makes the just person's death his assumption into heaven.[12]

A' (6:1-21) begins with an address to monarchs, informing them, like Psalm 2 and 82, that there is only one king, who will scrutinize the rule they have from him. By this point, the reader has heard about the nature of the world and about the role of wisdom and recognizes the relative nature of kings. Chapter 6:12-20 points forward to Part II (6:22–10:21) in its exhortation to attain wisdom. Jews in Alexandria liable to be awed by the splendors of Pharaonic Egypt and aware of the modest power of the Jewish community could take heart at the book's relativizing of kings and monarchs.

In summary, Part I (1:1–6:21) gives the "ontology" on which the ethics of the book is based. Despite appearances, the world ruled by kings and purposeless, violent people, "the wicked," is not the true and abiding reality. Another world coexists with it, animated by wisdom (or justice or the spirit of God), which is revealed only to those who seek wisdom and practice justice. The citizens of this world, "the children of God" who trust in their Father, are an affront to the ungodly party, for they witness to the other world. If they are killed by the ungodly, they will ascend to heaven and convict the ungodly of folly.

Part II (6:22–10:21): Wisdom and Its Way

Part II is the center of the book both structurally and conceptually. At this point, Wisdom of Solomon begins to speak directly about the animating principle of the true world, wisdom, and to show people how to attain it, and explain in detail how it directs the world. Fortunately, the ideas of Part II are less dense, or perhaps less alien to modern ways of thinking, than the ideas of Part I. Most of them can be communicated adequately through the outline I have provided.

Part II develops the ideas mentioned in Part I. Part I warned kings to seek wisdom, which is the animating principle of the true and eternal world. The real world is represented by loyal servants or "sons," who place their trust in God the creator and ruler of this world (chap. 2). Part II gives us an example of a king who genuinely sought wisdom his whole life, Solomon, though in keeping with the typifying tendency of wisdom literature it does not use his name. Further, chapter 10 begins to speak of specific servants of wisdom in history (again anonymously) and chapters 11 plus 16–19 identify Israel as that servant and son.

Here is an overview of Part II (6:22–10:21). Formally, chapters 7–8 are a single unit, for the material is united by the central chiasm diagrammed in the outline. Chapter 9 is the center of the book, the great prayer of Solomon, which points forward and backward, and chapter 10 is the list of the children of wisdom in Genesis, pointing forward to the guidance of wisdom in the exodus in chapters 12 plus 16–19.

Important points need to be highlighted in the units of Part II, 6:22–25, chapters 7–8, chapter 9, and chapter 10. The preface, 6:22–25, nicely introduces the main themes, though not in the order of their occurrence in the following chapters. The most important statement of Part II is made in the very first verse in the preface, 6:22, "I will tell you what wisdom is and how she came to be," but it is elaborated in the center of the chiasm, 7:2b–8:1. The last verse in the preface, verse 24, points forward to the other material in Part II. Verse 24a, "The multitude of the wise is the salvation of the world," introduces chapter 10 with its description of a succession

147

of wisdom-led heroes "saving" the world. Verse 24*b*, "A sensible king is the stability of any people," introduces the wise king of chapters 7–8.

The great chiasm in chapters 7–8 has as its center, 7:22*b*–8:1, the praise of wisdom. A detailed explanation follows. Its framework, the ABC / CBA sections in 6:22–8:21, is comparatively straightforward. A king speaks throughout. He emphasizes not his kingly status but his humanity so that he is a model to every human being. He tells us how he sought wisdom in preference to all other things (cf. Solomon's dream 1 Kgs 3:4-14). Wisdom is thus available to all who seek it from God. The comparison of the search for wisdom to the courting of a wife in chapter 8 develops traditions contained in Proverbs 1–9, especially chapter 8.

The unit in Part II that has aroused the most interest is 7:22*b*–8:1. Verses 22*b*-23 list twenty-one qualities of wisdom (three times seven), the most perfect number. In its form, the passage resembles aretalogies of Isis, lists of the miracles or virtues of the popular Egyptian goddess; they could be recited in the first or third person (as here). In the competition of religions in the Hellenistic age, such lists were useful in gaining converts. Wisdom seems to resemble most the Stoic world-spirit immanent in the universe. It permeates, unifies, and vivifies everything; it communicates virtue to intelligent creatures. Verses 25-26 contain a fivefold metaphor (the metaphors are italicized).

> For she is a *breath* of the power of God,
>   and a pure *emanation* of the glory of the Almighty;
>   therefore nothing defiled gains entrance into her.
> For she is a *reflection* of eternal light,
>   a spotless *mirror* of the working of God,
>   and an *image* of his goodness.

David Winston points out how bold the language is for someone writing within the biblical tradition.[15] Even the author's fellow Alexandrian philosopher Philo does not use such explicit terms as "emanation" or "reflection" for the origin of the Divine Logos. Verses 27-28 speak of Wisdom's governance of the world.

> Although she is but one, she can do all things,
>   and while remaining in herself, she renews all things;
>   in every generation she passes into holy souls

and makes them friends of God, and prophets;
for God loves nothing so much as the person who lives with wisdom.

Wisdom herself is unaffected as she affects others, a sign of transcendence and superiority. We learn that she not only ensures the cohesion and order of the universe and brings blessings to the human race. Her action is also interior; she is the principle of moral and religious life. She enters into certain people in every generation. The Bible generally designates selection as call or anointing, but Wisdom of Solomon views it as Wisdom entering a person. It is possible that the Q document of New Testament times, which is the source that scholars postulate for many passages in Matthew and Luke, understood this verse from Wisdom of Solomon to refer to Jesus as an emissary of Wisdom. Luke 7:35, "Wisdom is vindicated by all her children," might refer to this belief that Wisdom entered certain people in every age. At any rate, Wisdom of Solomon itself in chapter 10 points to such wisdom-inspired heroes in the book of Genesis. Wisdom has her own people in every age.

[29]She is more beautiful than the sun,
and excels every constellation of the stars.
Compared with the light she is found to be superior,
[30]for it is succeeded by the night,
but against wisdom evil does not prevail.
[8:1]She reaches mightily from one end of the earth to the other,
and she orders all things well.

The last verse may be a statement of Stoic cosmology, in which the movement of the world was caused by a continuous outward-inward movement of air from the center to the outermost pole. The sun imagery evokes Psalm 19, in which the rising of the sun is from the end of the heaven, and its circuit to the end of them, which becomes a metaphor for the word of God by which the world operates.

How are we to understand the figure of Wisdom? Is she a hypostasis in the sense of "a quasi-personification of certain attributes proper to God, occupying an intermediate position between personalities and abstract being"?[14] To interpret Wisdom as a hypothesis is inadequate, for, as M. Gilbert points out, the author would not place a mediator between God and creation, for that would not allow God any activity in the world. What is attributed to

149

Wisdom is attributed to God, on whom Wisdom utterly depends. Other scholars suggest simple personification of wisdom. But she is more than a literary figure. "The personification of Wisdom serves to express the action of God in the world, his presence to the universe, to human beings, in particular to the just."[15]

In chapter 9, which is the climax of Part II, the king prays for that wisdom that can only be given by God. Chapters 7–8 have established that "Solomon" is a human being as well as a king and thus his prayer is suitable for anyone. One suspects that the author has in mind the youth of Hellenistic Jewish communities who are reflecting on their future roles. The prayer is in three sections, verses 1-6, 7-12, and 13-18, which have as topics, respectively, human beings, king, and human beings. Each section contains a prayer for wisdom, verses 4, 10, and 17. Wisdom is closely associated, if not identified, with God's word (v. 2) and God's spirit (v. 17).

How does the great prayer, and indeed the whole of Part II, fit into the argument of Wisdom of Solomon up to this point? The very first chapter of the book commanded the kings of the world to seek wisdom above all else in view of a future divine judgment. Despite appearances it is wisdom that rules the true and abiding world. The true world has its own adherents, the just who are recognizable by their obedience and childlike trust in God the creator. Solomon fits this scenario. He is a king who indeed seeks wisdom and a just person who prays for wisdom and behaves as a child or servant of God. In chapter 2, the wicked say that the righteous person "professes to have knowledge of God, and calls himself a child of the Lord" (v. 13), and "boasts that God is his father," and "if the righteous man is God's child, he will help him." "Solomon" is that righteous man as well as the king. The identification of the anonymous citizens of the true world sketched in Part I (1:1–6:21) as Israel in Part II sets the stage for the reinterpretation of Israel's history in chapter 10 (Genesis) and especially chapters 12 plus 16–19 (Exodus). Israel itself is the child of God, "[The Egyptians] acknowledged your people to be God's child" (18:13).

Chapter 10 is the bridge between the praise of wisdom in Part II and the exposition of wisdom's role in human history. The prayer of Solomon in the preceding chapter began with wisdom in creation (9:1-3) and ended with wisdom in history and its redemption, "and thus the paths of those on earth were set right, / and people were taught what pleases you, / and were saved by wisdom." The last point, human beings being saved by wisdom, is illustrated by seven ancestors whose histories are told in the books of Genesis and Exodus. The first three, Adam, Cain (and Abel), and Noah are non-Israelites. The last four, Abraham, Lot, Jacob, Joseph are ancestors of Israel. The seventh wisdom-hero, Moses, is mentioned in 10:15–11:1-4 and forms the transition to the reinterpretation of the great saving event that leads to the formation of Israel, the Exodus. Wisdom is the agent throughout the chapter, delivering Adam from transgression, getting rid of Cain, saving the world "by a paltry piece of wood" (Noah), protecting Abraham from the Gentiles, saving Lot and punishing the Sodomites, guiding Jacob, making his flocks abundant and protecting him, raising up Moses and protecting the people through him. These individuals from biblical history are types of the "child" of God who is a citizen not of this world but of the other. Their lives show us how wisdom "saves" the world (9:18), in every generation "passing into holy souls" (7:27). With the mention of Moses and the exodus we come to Part III.

Part III (11:1–19:22): The Exodus

The exodus of the children of Israel from the land of Egypt and their entry into the land of Canaan is the greatest event recorded in the Hebrew Bible. In biblical tradition, it is the most dramatic act of God in history, and it is the formation or creation of the people of Israel. In that event they are given a land to possess really and not simply in promise, they are given God's new name Yahweh and thus a new and definitive relationship with him, they are given a leader, Moses, legal and narrative traditions, and a house for their God. These elements, God, land, leader, traditions, are what made a people in the ancient world. The exodus is the creation of Israel. No wonder that the author of Wisdom of Solomon devotes the bulk of the book to this central event!

Retelling the events of biblical history was common among Jewish writers in the Hellenistic age, for example, Pseudo-Philo, Ben Sira, and the book of Jubilees. These authors did not, however, simply summarize; they recast the stories for their own rhetorical ends. Ben Sira in chapters 44–50 looked upon Israel's history as the actions of certain great men, "Let us now praise famous men." Wisdom of Solomon recasts the entire exodus as the plagues! The author takes each plague and shows how God made its element (such as water, light, flies, and locusts) work *against* the Egyptians and *for* Israel. The comparison of two things, called *synkrisis* in the Greek rhetoric of the time, was a common way of arguing. A Greek speaker could compare, for example, the customs of the Spartans and the customs of the Athenians, in order to clarify what was special to each. So also with Israel and the Egyptians.

What is the relation of the exodus to the earlier part of the book? The earlier part declared that God ruled the world by wisdom and protected his servants. Part III shows how this was done in the time of the exodus. God changed the elements of the world to protect the loyal "child" Israel and punished Egypt as he punished the violent aggressors of chapter 2 in the great judgment scene of chapter 5.

There are two digressions or excursus in the final part, both related to the theme of the exodus. The first is on God as a purposeful and merciful teacher of the enemies of Israel at the time of the exodus, the Canaanites and the Egyptians. These enemies stand for the wicked schemers in Part I, who were offended by the loyal child of God and planned to kill him (chap. 2). The excursus shows how God punishes them in this life and to what end. The second excursus is a critique of religions of the period, the religion of the philosophers, idolatry, and zoolatry (the worship of animals), practiced by the Egyptians.

Excursus I (11:15–12:27) God as Teacher and Reprover. It is wise to begin with formal observations. There are two units, followed by a double conclusion. The first unit is 11:15–12:2, and has its center and argument of principle in 11:20*d*, "But you have arranged all things by measure and number and weight." In the context of the excursus, this principle means that God punishes with great moderation and that the punishment has as its aim the correction and repentance of the sinner, for God loves all that he has made and does not desire any being's destruction (11:23-26; cf. 1:13-14). Verse 16 states an important biblical principle regarding divine judgment, the correspondence of sin and punishment: the punishment fits the crime, one is punished by the very things by which one sins.

The second unit presents a second consideration, parallel to the first (12:3-18): God was moderate toward the benighted Canaanites, sending them wasps to lead them to repentance rather than wipe them all out by an army (12:8-10). Verses 19-22 apply this principle to Israel, and the concluding verses 23-27 restate the principle of correspondence of sin to punishment and state the ultimate penalty for hardened hearts (12:27*d*).

Excursus II (13:1–15:19) A Critique of Other Philosophies and

152

Religions. The author's analysis of the philosophy and religion of the day is in essence a critique of Hellenistic culture, which posed a danger to the Jewish community, especially to its youth. The critique is not friendly; it is not a course in world religions but an attack on competing religions and philosophies. The Hellenistic age was a marketplace of ideas, in which proponents of a way of life showed its superiority to other ways, and that is the purpose of this unit.

The best guide to the entire excursus is the outline of the book I have given, especially the chiasm structuring the second and longest subunit, on image worship (13:10–15:13). Rather than go through the arguments, which are not difficult, I will offer a few comments on some important points. In 13:1-19, the author criticizes philosophers (especially Stoics) not for denying the existence of the divine but for failing to distinguish God from God's manifestations. They divinized the elements of the world and thus were unable to find the God who is distinct from them. The subunit on idolatry draws on biblical texts such as Deuteronomy 4:27-28; Psalms 115:3-8; 135:15-18; Isaiah 40:18-20; 44:9-20; 46:1-7; Jeremiah 10:2-16, which satirized divine images in order to encourage the worship of Israel's unique God. It is built around a chiasm, which is the best clue to its meaning. In the terminology of the outline, subunits a and a' (13:10-19; 15:7-13) analyze the intentions of idol-makers. The centerpiece (14:11-31) tells how idol worship started and details its pernicious consequences. Within the chiasm there are matching subunits that contrast idolatry to biblical history (14:1-10; 15:1-6).

The Seven Comparisons (11:6-14 + 16–19). Biblical history is retold in a way that is meaningful for the present generation of Jews living in Egypt and other diaspora communities. The central event of Israel's history, the exodus, would have been familiar to any Jew from its central place in the Passover meal and from other citations. The exodus is viewed as seven miracles, transformations of natural events and elements in favor of the holy people and against their enemies, the Egyptians. The retelling is richly detailed and full of surprising elaborations.

The best approach is to read the comparisons using the outline supplied in this chapter. Some features can be pointed out. The first and last verses (11:1 and 19:22) give the principle of interpretation, "[Wisdom] prospered their works by the hand of a holy prophet," and "For in everything, O Lord, you have exalted and glorified your people, / and you have not neglected to help them at all times and in all places." The story is basically one: God literally moves heaven and earth to keep his people safe from their enemies and to glorify them in the sight of their enemies. This very specific goal explains the unusual interpretation of the exodus as the plagues (rather than, say, the giving of the law or entering the land of promise). In each plague God makes use of the elements to punish the wicked and protect the righteous. God is depicted as Lord of the universe, for example, "For creation, serving you who made it, / exerts itself to punish the unrighteous, / and in kindness relaxes on behalf of those who trust in you" (16:24); "For the whole creation in its nature was fashioned anew, / complying with your commands, / so that your children might be kept unharmed" (19:6). The mention of "children" brings the reader back to Part I, where the child of God enraged the wicked with his trust in God (chap. 2) and was finally raised up by God as his persecutors looked on in utter confusion (chap. 5). In short, the seven comparisons in Part III simply extend to the history of the people of Israel the individual drama played out in chapters 2–5.

THE MEANING OF WISDOM OF SOLOMON TODAY

The Wisdom of Solomon is a thoroughly biblical wisdom book and a work of Hellenistic philosophy and religion. Can the Wisdom of Solomon as a book of the past speak to our time?

I suggest there are two affirmations that still ring especially true today. The first is that God is Lord of the universe, consisting not only of heaven and earth but of nature and history. Many modern believers instinctively make God the Lord of heaven but implicitly retreat from God's affirming lordship of earth, nature, and history. Such people have difficulty seeing God at work in the world, in human history, and are disposed to think separately of God in history and in nature. Wisdom of Solomon affirms the central reality of God the creator and of God's choice of Israel. God acts in history (in the book's perspective) primarily by dealing with Israel, in which work he reshapes at will human activity and natural elements. "For the elements changed places with one another, / as on a harp the notes vary the nature of the rhythm, / while each note remains the same" (19:18). God's rule is called his wisdom. It must be sought in prayer, preferred to all else, and yet, paradoxically, is conferred as a gift. Its possession enables one to see the true nature of reality and to remain faithful.

Second, the Lord's rule is hidden in that it has not yet appeared in its fullness. There are, therefore, "two worlds." The two worlds of Wisdom of Solomon correspond to the two ways of ancient wisdom literature. One world is all too familiar, for its law is "Might makes right" and the weak are at risk from violent and selfish people. It is ruled over by the kings of this world. The other world has not yet appeared, but it is eternal, for it is ruled by God. Each world has its party, its citizens. The citizens of this world are doomed because their world is passing away, but the citizens of the true world have eternal life.

The real world is marked by life and the other world is marked by death. Paradoxically, it is when the righteous are faithful and rescued that the real world appears. In Part I, the death of the (typical) righteous person who trusts in God shows forth the true world when God raises him up in the sight of those who killed him. In Part III, the nature of God is shown forth in the rescue of the "child" of God, Israel. As they are rescued in the sight of the Egyptians, the latter know they are wrong. The true world is revealed in the trusting and obedient conduct of the chosen ones.

RECOMMENDED READING

Commentaries

Kolarcik, Michael. "The Book of Wisdom," in *The New Interpreter's Bible,* vol. 5. Nashville: Abingdon Press, 1997. Pp. 435-600. Well informed and judicious.

Reese, James M. *The Book of Wisdom, Song of Songs.* Old Testament Message. Wilmington: Glazier, 1983. Concise and informed.

———. "The Wisdom of Solomon" in *Harper's Bible Commentary.* San Francisco: Harper, 1988. Pp. 820-35. Brief but excellent.

Reider, J. *The Book of Wisdom. An English Translation with Commentary.* New York: Harper, 1957.

Winston, David. *The Wisdom of Solomon.* Anchor Bible 43. Garden City, N.Y.: Doubleday, 1979. Erudite, keen analysis, comprehensive.

Wright, Addison G. "Wisdom," in *NJBC,* 510-22. Interesting on structure.

Special Studies

Collins, John J. *Jewish Wisdom in the Hellenistic Age.* Old Testament Library. Louisville: Westminster John Knox, 1997, 133-57, 178-221.

Kolarcik, Michael. *The Ambiguity of Death in the Book of Wisdom 1-6: A Study of Literary Structure and Interpretation.* Analecta Biblica 127. Rome: Biblical Institute, 1991.

Nickelsburg, George. *Resurrection, Immortality, and Eternal Life in Intertestamental Judaism.* Harvard Theological Studies 26. Cambridge: Harvard, 1972.

CHAPTER 8

THE SONG OF SONGS

The Song of Songs (Song of Solomon) is, despite the singular title, a collection of songs. "Song of Songs" is a superlative in Hebrew, like "vanity of vanities" for "the most absurd," and "holy of holies" for "the most holy." In the standard Hebrew Bible the Song takes up ten and a half pages, compared with nineteen pages for Qoheleth and fifty-four for Proverbs.

The songs are not poems *about* lovers but poems *by* lovers, a man and a woman, or, given the likely age of the pair (mid or late teens), two very young adults. The speakers can be identified as male or female by the feminine and masculine second-person singular verb and suffix forms and by the feminine and masculine forms of adjectives. The Hebrew of 2:10, for example, "Arise, my love, my beautiful one, and come away," is addressed by the man to the woman, for it has feminine singular markers.

Though the Song must be read as the lyric poetry that it is, it comes from another time and place and requires careful study to appreciate its style, conventions, and subject matter. The important issues are its date and social context, its genre and comparable literature, its literary structure, and the poetic world of the texts.

THE DATE AND SOCIAL CONTEXT

The Song contains no allusion to any datable historical event. It is ascribed to King Solomon (1:1) on the basis of the occurrence of his name in 1:5; 4:7; 8:11-12, but these are foils against which the lovers are portrayed. According to 1 Kings 5:12 (EV 4:32), Solomon was a composer of songs, and according to 1 Kings 11 he was a great lover, including many foreign women and a royal princess from Egypt. The royal references do not imply Solomon was the author, for it is conventional for lovers to give each other royal titles as in 1:4, 12; 7:6; and 6:8, 9. The mention in 6:4 of Tirzah, the capital of the northern kingdom in the tenth to ninth centuries, is no indication of date, but simply a balance in the same verse to Jerusalem, the capital of the southern kingdom; it plays on the triliteral root "to please."

The only reliable criterion for dating is the language, which resembles Mishnaic Hebrew in some of its vocabulary, constructions, and syntactical usages. The most striking late Hebrew usage is the consistent use of the relative particle *šě* instead of the *'ăšer* of classical biblical Hebrew. The language shows the work to be postexilic, composed probably between the fourth and second centuries B.C.E. As Michael Fox especially has shown, there is an extraordinarily close relationship of the Song to Egyptian love lyrics of the nineteenth and early twentieth dynasties (ca. 1305–ca. 1150). Common themes and word usage suggest the Song grew from the much earlier Egyptian models, though we cannot fill in the thousand-year gap between the Egyptian love lyrics and the Song.[1]

The Song gives no information about its origin or the context in which it was performed. It may have been part of the entertainment provided at a banquet. Banqueters are a suitable audience, as Fox notes, for the Song "is full of fun, erotic allusions, sensual word-paintings of the lovers and their worlds, and heart-warming sentiments."[2] Some scholars suggest a marriage celebration on the basis of the wedding procession mentioned in 3:6-11, but the Song does not indicate this. Whatever the context, it was one marked by joyous receptivity to the lyrics of two lovers boldly seeking and happily finding each other.

How did love lyrics composed for public performance find their way into the canon of sacred writings? Some suggest that the Song was simply part of the entertainment of the banquets that were common during religious holidays in Judaism. It became "sacred" simply by being associated with the religious festivals. Only later, when it had become a text of the festivals, did it receive a religious interpretation.[5] The explanation may be correct as far as it goes, but it leaves unexplained why the Song was taken into the canon of *sacred* scripture. Whatever the details, the Song must have been recognized as beautiful in itself and therefore an apt expression of the relation of Yahweh and Israel as lovers.

GENRE AND COMPARABLE LITERATURE

The genre of the Song is love poetry, lyrical utterances of a man and a woman to each other and at times with others. The best way of treating the forms and conventions of the love poetry is to read the Song with a knowledge of its conventions. Its nearest nonbiblical analogues are the Egyptian love songs of the nineteenth and twentieth dynasties, which have been published in Fox's *Song of Songs*.[4] Two excerpts follow, which show some of the metaphors and conventions found in the Song.

(Woman)
(A) The voice of the dove speaks. It says:
　　"Day has dawned—
　　　　when are you going (home)?"
(B) Stop it, bird!
　　　　you're teasing(?) me.
　　I found my brother in his bedroom,
　　　　and my heart was exceedingly joyful.
(C) We say (to each other):
　　　　"I will never be far away.
　　(My) hand will be with (your) hand,
　　　　as I stroll about.
　　I with (you),
　　　　in every pleasant place."
(D) He regards me as the best of the beautiful,
　　　　and has not wounded my heart.

The woman chides the dove for announcing the dawn that ends the night of love. She tells how she went looking for her lover and found him in his bedroom, and she then quotes their declarations of love.[5]

(Man)
(A) One alone is (my) sister, having no peer:
    more gracious than all other women.
(B) Behold her, like Sothis rising
    at the beginning of a good year:
  shining, precious, white of skin,
    lovely of eyes <when> gazing.
(C) Sweet her lips when speaking:
    she has no excess of words.
  Long of neck, white of breast,
    her hair true lapis lazuli.
(D) Her arms surpass gold,
    her fingers are like lotuses.
  Full(?) (her) derrière, narrow(?) (her) waist,
    her thighs carry on her beauties.
  Lovely of <walk> when she strides on the ground,
    she has captured my heart in her embrace.[6]

The man sees the woman walking along the street and praises her in his thought. In the next stanzas the man and the woman speak about an event in their lives from a single point of view, even though they do not follow chronological order.

THE LITERARY STRUCTURE

A central question is whether the Song is a single poem with a relatively small number of parts, or a collection of poems. If the first option is taken, is the unity sequential (a drama) or schematic (an artistic arrangement)? Scholarly estimates of the units in the Song range from five to fifty! Those who agree on one of the two options may not agree on the demarcation of units.

What is the best way to speak of literary structure in the face of such diverse opinion? Given the purpose of this series, to help readers into the world of the text rather than survey scholarly opinion, the outline given here is by design shorter than most (only twelve units) and will form the basis of comments in the next section. It makes use of a "she and he" approach on the basis of Hebrew markers. The titles highlight the main themes and can facilitate an initial reading.

1. 1:2-4. She: The kisses of his mouth
2. 1:5-8. She: Search on a sunny afternoon. Chorus or he: v. 8

3. 1:9–2:7. Duet. He: 9-11, 15, 2:2. She: 12-14, 16-17, 2:1, 3-7
4. 2:8-17. The surprise of spring. (Monologue of the woman, citing the man in vv. 10-15.) She: 2:8-9, 16-17; He: 10-15
5. 3:1-5. The night in the city. She
6. 3:6-11. Chorus: The sedan chair of Solomon
7. 4:1–5:1. The song of the body. He: 4:1-15, 5:1. She: 4:16
8. 5:2–6:3. The night of absence. She: 5:2-8, 10-17, 6:2-3. Chorus: 5:9, 6:1
9. 6:4–7:10. The new song of the body. He: 6:4-12, 7:2-10. Chorus: 7:1
10. 7:11–8:4. In the vineyard. She
11. 8:5-7. Place me as a seal. She: 5b-7. Chorus: 8a
12. 8:8-14. Wall and vine. Chorus: 8:8-9. She: 10, 14. He: 11-13.

The outline leaves open the question whether the Song is a unity or a loose collection. There is no completely convincing evidence either that the Song has a literary structure (sequential or schematic) or that it is an anthology of diverse pieces. One way out of the dilemma is to attend to the unifying devices at work in the poem. Their effect is to make the Song a unified poem in the sense that its characters are the same throughout and their speeches all speak of the same "event" (their love) from different points of view.[7]

One unifying factor is its network of recurrent phrases and sentences in different parts of the book. A good example is 8:14 (woman), which repeats 4:6b (man); and 2:17b (woman).

8:14 (Woman)	4:6b (Man)	2:17b (Woman)
Make haste, my beloved, and be like a gazelle		Turn, my beloved, be like a gazelle,
or a young stag upon the mountains of spices!	I will hasten to the mountain of myrrh and the hill of frankincense.	or a young stag on the cleft mountains.
		2:9a (Woman) My beloved is like a gazelle or a young stag.

161

Other examples are 8:11-12 (Man), which picks up 1:6*b* (Woman); 8:5*a*, which picks up 3:6*a*.

The second unifying device is what Fox calls associative sequences, words, sentences, or motifs, which recur in the same order even though that order is not required from the narrative context. Examples are the phrase "How beautiful you are, my darling," in 4:1*a* and 1:15*ab*, both followed by "Your eyes are doves." A more complex example is the sequence of motifs in 8:2-5, which parallels the sequence in 3:4*b*-6*a* and 2:6-7. The last indication of unity is the narrative frame—the season is summer throughout the poem.

The conclusion is that the Song is not merely an anthology (there is too much unity for that), but neither is it one tightly knit poem. It is rather a coherent poetic work with changes of scene, discrete episodes, some very clear breaks (e.g., 5:2 and 6:4), yet telling a single story.

THE POETIC WORLD OF THE TEXTS

How different is the logic of the Song from that in the wisdom literature examined so far! The Song is not communicating ideas, forming character, or examining great human problems. Lyric poetry expresses the love, longing, anxiety, and yearning of lovers to each other and to their circle. A different approach is called for. Rather than analyze the poems, I provide here guidance to the world of the texts.

In lyric poetry, the speaker is usually a first-person singular voice, an I-speaker, and has an intense relationship to the subject. The audience the I-speaker addresses can vary—the beloved, a friend, a stranger, God, even the self. Marcia Falk identifies several types of lyrics in the poem.[8]

1) The "love monologue" by an I-speaker addressed to, or about, the beloved. More than half the poems in the book fall under this heading: 1:2-4, 9-11, 12-14; 2:16-17; 3:1-5; 4:1-7, 8, 9-11; 6:4-10, 11; 7:7-10, 11-14; 8:1-4, 5*b*, 6-7.

2) The "love dialogue" as a conversation between two lovers. Examples are 1:7-8, 15-17; 2:1-3, 8-13; 4:12–5:1; 8:13-14.

3) A monologue spoken by an I-speaker in a love relationship to an audience outside that relationship, for example, 1:5-6 and 8:11-12. There may be other speakers and a variety of audiences.

The classification helps one to see the shifts in the speakers and in those addressed. The Song is not simply set speeches.

Another consideration in the song is the physical context in which the lovers are found. Drawing on Falk again,[9] we find that there are four basic contexts, (1) the cultivated or habitable countryside; (2) the wild or remote natural landscape; (3) interior environments such as houses, hall, and rooms; (4) city streets. Each context contributes to the mood. The love dialogues take place in the countryside (1), where the beauty and fruitfulness of the landscape supports the positive statements. Nature can also be remote, wild, or even perilous (2), and such regions mirror the mysterious, elusive, and sometimes dangerous side of loving relationships. Interior spaces (3) are where the love-making takes place. Among indoor spaces, the mother's house is a place of refuge from the hostility of the crowded streets. The city streets (4) are the place least welcoming to the lovers. There the woman meets the hostile city guards, and there she meets the sometimes incredulous and scornful women of the city.

In addition to sensitivity to speaker and audience, and to physical setting, modern readers will be helped by knowing the principal themes, which recur (in different formulations) in the poem. Falk identifies the most frequent: (1) inviting the beloved, (2) banishing the beloved, (3) searching for the beloved, (4) the self in a hostile world, and (5) praise of love itself.[10] Here following is an illustration of each.

1) Inviting the beloved is age-old. The yearning of the lovers for each other is deep and can be expressed in dozens of ways, as in the opening lines, 1:2, "Let him kiss me with the kisses of his mouth! / For your love is better than wine" or 2:10, "Arise, my love, my fair one, and come away; / for now the winter is past, / the rain is over and gone." She invites him to come near.

2) The theme of banishing the beloved arises from caution, for not everyone favors their love. One lover can tell the other to flee until there is a more opportune time of encounter, as in 2:17, "Turn, my beloved, be like a gazelle, / or a young stag on the cleft mountains." Their love can be fully expressed only when they are alone.

3) Searching for the beloved. The language of losing and finding recurs throughout the poem, for the experience of lovers is not simply finding and enjoying complete rest. They rather find and lose and find again. This is the authentic rhythm of life, and it

163

provides much of the drama and tension of the Song. "Upon my bed at night / I sought him whom my soul loves; / I sought him, but found him not; . . . / I will rise now and go about the city, / in the streets and in the squares" (3:1-2).

4) The self in a hostile world. Both lovers assert themselves strongly, for love enables them to be their authentic selves. An example is the encounter with the girls of Jerusalem in 1:5-7: "I am black and beautiful, / O daughters of Jerusalem, / like the tents of Kedar, / like the curtains of Solomon. / Do not gaze at me because I am dark, / because the sun has gazed on me. / My mother's sons were angry with me; / they made me keeper of the vineyards, / but my own vineyard I have not kept!" The woman is dark from the sun because her brothers have forced her to work in the field. She does not have the pale skin that was thought beautiful, so the other girls taunt her. Her brothers will show themselves hostile to her in 8:8-10.

5) Praise of love itself. It is not surprising that one intoxicated by love should sing its praises, and this the woman does in 7:6-9 and 8:6-7, "Set me as a seal upon your heart, / as a seal upon your arm; / for love is strong as death, / passion fierce as the grave."

With this provisional outline, and with a sense of the recurring themes and motifs in mind, the reader should be able to understand the Song, and, more important, to enjoy it.

RECOMMENDED READING

Commentaries

Falk, Marcia. *The Song of Songs: A New Translation and Interpretation.* San Francisco: Harper, 1990. Has a poet's sensitivity both in the very free translation and in the commentary.

Fox, Michael. *The Song of Songs and the Ancient Egyptian Love Songs.* Madison: University of Wisconsin, 1985. Fresh translation of and notes on the Egyptian love poetry and the Song.

Gordis, Robert. *The Song of Songs and Lamentations.* New York: KTAV, 1974.

Keel, Othmar, *The Song of Songs.* Continental Commentary. Minneapolis: Fortress, 1994. Up-to-date; especially valuable for its attention to ancient art and iconography.

Murphy, Roland E. *The Song of Songs.* Hermeneia. Minneapolis:

Fortress, 1990. Learned and detailed, a balanced and judicious presentation.

Pope, Marvin. *Song of Songs*. Anchor Bible 7C. Garden City, N.Y.: Doubleday, 1977. Both a commentary and a great repository of exotica and erotica.

Tournay, Raymond J. *Word of God, Song of Love*. New York: Paulist, 1988. Attends to both the lyrical and allegorical sides of the book.

Weems, Renita J. "The Song of Songs," in *The New Interpreter's Bible*. Vol. 5. Nashville: Abingdon Press, 1997. Pp. 361-434.

Special Studies

Astell, Ann W. *The Song of Songs in the Middle Ages*. Ithaca, N.Y.: Cornell University, 1990.

Brenner, Athalya, ed. *A Feminist Companion to the Song of Songs*. Sheffield: JSOT, 1993. A collection of essays on the Song.

Exum, J. Cheryl. "A Literary and Structural Analysis of the Song of Songs," *ZAW* 85 (1973): 46-79. Elaborate argument for a schematic structure.

Matter, E. Ann. *The Voice of My Beloved: The Song of Songs in Western Medieval Christianity*. Philadelphia: University of Pennsylvania, 1990.

Murphy, Roland E. "Interpreting the Song of Songs," *BTB* 9 (1979): 99-105.

Trible, Phyllis. "Love's Lyrics Redeemed," in *God and the Rhetoric of Sexuality*. Philadelphia: Fortress, 1978. Pp. 144-65.

CHAPTER 9

WISDOM IN JUDAISM AND CHRISTIANITY

B y design, this book has concentrated on "the world of the text," rather than on scholarly issues such as the dates of the books, their social world, the wisdom traditions and their history, or the development of the themes and rhetoric after Wisdom of Solomon. Yet a brief word must be said in this final chapter on what happened to wisdom literature in Judaism and early Christianity.

Wisdom was a very powerful current in late Second-Temple Judaism and in early Christianity, as has been increasingly recognized in the last two decades. The most recent of the quests for the historical Jesus is very much interested in Jesus as a wise man who drew upon the biblical wisdom literature and used its methods. To some scholars, Jesus was primarily a sage, engaging people by his instructions, sayings, and parables.[1] In addition, the Qumran scrolls show there was a considerable amount of interest in wisdom literature and related themes in this Jewish sect, and beyond the confines of Qumran.[2]

JUDAISM

Palestinian Judaism of the last Second Temple period witnessed the writing of the Wisdom of Ben Sira, in which the wisdom stream broadened to include historical traditions (Sirach 44–50) and commentary on earlier written Scripture (Sirach 24 on Proverbs 8). Baruch 3:9–4:4 alludes to Job 28 and Sirach 24 to show that the rulers of nations never found Wisdom, unlike Israel who finds it in the book of the commandments of the law (4:1). In Hellenistic Judaism, the Wisdom of Solomon makes a similar use of the historical traditions (Wisdom 10–19) and also revisits old wisdom texts (as well as other texts), but with a view shaped by non-Jewish philosophy. One work that is particularly influenced by wisdom books is *Pirqe Abot,* the Sayings of the Fathers, a collection of sayings from the "men of the Great Assembly" (between the late-fifth and the third centuries B.C.E.) down to the descendants of Rabbi Judah the Prince in the third century C.E. It is one of the treatises in the Mishnah, where it became the object of commentary in *Abot de Rabbi Nathan.* Its opening sentence places the men of the Great Assembly in a line, from Moses to Joshua, the elders, and the prophets. The wisdom text of the Cairo Geniza, which some date with the first century C.E. Hebrew ethical wills, in which parents hand on to their children their wisdom, were influenced by the wisdom instruction.

THE NEW TESTAMENT

Early Christians saw Jesus as a wisdom teacher and employed the tradition of personified wisdom to express his incarnation. Among various influences on the New Testament was the theme of wisdom hidden with God yet revealed to human beings, the identification of wisdom with divine spirit, word, and law. The forms of instruction, admonition, and paradoxical saying continued to be used.

The Letter of James draws on the instruction form. The Letter is a series of instructions using the familiar exhortatory verbs (imperatives, jussives) followed by reasons, which are often sayings or proverbs. Familiar themes appear: the danger of an unbridled tongue (chap. 3; cf. Prov 10:18-21), of presumptuous planning (4:13-17; cf. Prov 16:1), and of ill-gotten wealth (5:1-6; cf. Prov

10:2-3). Though down-to-earth like Proverbs, James nonetheless exalts "wisdom from above" (3:13-18 and cf. 1:17), invoking the topos of wisdom beyond the reach of human beings but graciously given to them (Proverbs 8, Job 28, and Sirach 24). The wisdom instruction does not remain unchanged, however, for James adds his own contribution—prophetic denunciations of the callous rich (1:27; 2:1-13; 4:1-10; 5:1-6).

Paul's argument against those who are scandalized by the cross in 1 Corinthians 1:17-2:13 reshapes in a sharp paradox the traditional antithesis between the wise and the foolish as well as that between human and divine wisdom found in Job 28 and Proverbs 8: "For since, in the wisdom of God, the world did not know God through wisdom, God decided, through the foolishness of our proclamation, to save those who believe" (1 Cor 1:21).

Wisdom traditions influenced the putative written source of the Synoptic Gospels Matthew and Luke—Q (for *Quelle,* German for "source"). Most scholars believe that Q emphasized Jesus' teachings rather than his death and resurrection. The strength of wisdom themes is illustrated by a Q saying in Matthew 11:27 (parallel Luke 10:22): "All things have been handed over to me by my Father, and no one knows the Son except the Father; and no one knows the Father except the Son and anyone to whom the Son wishes to reveal him." The saying is part of the Jewish and early Christian debate about what and where wisdom is. Is Wisdom to be identified with the law (Sirach 24), heavenly mysteries (*1 Enoch* 42:1-3), or Christ (Col 1:15-20; John 1:1-18)? Is she to be found in the Jerusalem Temple (Sir 24:8-12), everywhere in the cosmos (Wis 7:24-26), in heaven (*1 Enoch* 42:1-3), or in the church (Col 1:18)? Jesus in the text is divine wisdom incarnate, for to know him is to know the Father who is wisdom itself. The immediately following verses, 11:28-30 (unique to Matthew), "Come to me, all you that are weary and are carrying heavy burdens, and I will give you rest. Take my yoke upon you, and learn from me," echo Sirach 51:23-30, Ben Sira's invitation to attend his school and become his disciple. Matthew therefore answers the question of the early debate—Wisdom is found in Jesus and his teaching.

Of all the Gospels, John is the most persistent in regarding Jesus as incarnate wisdom descended from on high to offer human beings life and truth.[3] The Gospel expresses Jesus' heavenly origin by identifying him with personified Wisdom. As Woman Wisdom was with God from the beginning, even before the creation of the world (Prov 8:22-23; Sir 24:9; Wis 6:22), so Jesus is the Word in the beginning (1:1), and with the Father before the world existed (17:5). As Wisdom teaches human beings heavenly secrets (Job 11:6-7; Wis 9:16-18) and shows them how to walk in the way that leads to life (Prov 2:20-22; 3:13-26; 8:32-35; Sir 4:12) and immortality (Wis 6:18-19), so Jesus functions as revealer in John. Jesus speaks in long discourses like Woman Wisdom (Prov 1:20-33; 8). Wisdom invites people to partake of her rich banquet, where the food and drink symbolize life and closeness to God (Prov 9:2-5; Sir 24:19-21). Jesus does the same: "I am the bread of life. Whoever comes to me will never be hungry, and whoever believes in me will never be thirsty" (6:35 and cf. Prov 9:1-6 + 11). As Wisdom seeks friends (Prov 1:20-21; 8:1-4; Wis 6:16), so Jesus recruits followers (1:36-38, 43).

Two early Christian hymns identify Jesus with God's creative word and with heavenly wisdom: John 1:1-18 and Colossians 1:15-20. The Greek word *logos,* "word" in John 1 refers both to wisdom and to word as they are used in the Old Testament. Sirach 24:3 ("From the mouth of the Most High I came forth") and Wisdom 9:1-2 had already associated wisdom and word. Wisdom 7:22 says Wisdom is unique *(monogenēs)* and the prologue says the Word is God's unique *(monogenēs)* son. Wisdom sets up her tent in Sirach 24:8 as does Jesus in John 1:14 *(eskēnenosen,* "to tent"). In Sirach 24:16 Wisdom has glory *(doxa)* and grace *(charis)* like Jesus in John 1:14.

The hymn about creation in Colossians 1:15-20 applies to Christ the creative role of Wisdom.

> [15]He is the image of the invisible God,
>   the firstborn of all creation.
> [16]For in him all things in heaven and earth were created
> . . . .
> [18]He is the head of the body, the church;
>   he is the beginning, the firstborn from the dead. (NRSV, adapted)

Like John 1, the hymn combines the traditions of creative word and wisdom from Proverbs 8 and Wisdom 7. Creation and redemption are placed in parallel. Verses 15-17 affirm that Christ was the model when the human race was created (created in the image of God, Gen 1:27-28) and is now the model for the new creation.

NOTES

2. WISDOM LITERATURE IN THE ANCIENT NEAR EAST

1. See the concise survey by J. J. M. Roberts, "The Bible and the Literature of Antiquity: The Ancient Near East," in *Harper's Bible Commentary* (San Francisco: Harper, 1988), 33-41.

2. For a summary of the question, see R. Clifford, *Creation Accounts in the Ancient Near East and in the Bible* CBQMS 26 (Washington: Catholic Biblical Association, 1994), 74-82, 144-50.

3. The concept of genre, or "type" or "form," has always been controversial. Until the eighteenth century, it was taken prescriptively, but now descriptively. A great problem is how to avoid the hermeneutic circle: how can one choose specific examples of a genre unless one already knows what the genre is. See "Genre" in Alex Preminger and T. V. F. Brogan, eds., *The New Princeton Encyclopedia of Poetry and Poetics* (Princeton: Princeton University, 1993), 456-58.

4. This sketch is drawn from C. Wilcke, "Göttliche und menschliche Weisheit im Alten Orient," in *Weisheit: Archäologie der literarischen Kommunikation III*, A. Assman, ed. (Munich: Fink, 1991), 259-70.

5. W. G. Lambert, *BWL* (Oxford: Clarendon, 1960), 1.

6. *BWL*, 275.

7. A partial translation is in *ANET*, 594-95. Full translations are in *TUAT* 3.1. I am translating the German of Römer, who renders the Old Babylonian Sumerian text.

8. "Near" seems to correspond to English "to speak rashly."

9. Römer observes that the image means that not only a daughter is addressed.

10. The translation is from *BM*, 328-31. Some translations and comments are drawn from Lambert, *BWL*, 96-107.

11. *TUAT*, vol. 1, pp. 24-30, 33. I translate from the German.

12. The following remarks on Mesopotamian scribes owe much to A. Leo Oppenheim, "The Position of the Intellectual in Mesopotamian Society," *Daedelus* 104 (1975): 37-45.

13. The following remarks owe much to H. Brunner, *Die Weisheitsbücher der Ägypter* (Zürich: Artemis, 1991), 11-98.

14. On *maat* and the Bible, see M. V. Fox, "World Order and Ma'at: A Crooked Parallel," *Journal of the Ancient Near Eastern Society* 23 (1995): 37-48.

15. *AEL*, vol. 2, p. 149. Cf. *ANET,* 421-22.

16. *AEL*, vol. 1, p. 64.

17. *AEL*, vol. 2, p. 152.

18. Trans. J. M. Lindenberger, *The Old Testament Pseudepigrapha,* vol. 2 (Garden City, N.Y.: Doubleday, 1985), 479-507. The underlining means uncertain restoration.

19. Only one saying (6.82-83), "Spare not your son from the rod, otherwise, can / you save him [from *wickedness*]? / If I beat you, my son, / you will not die; / but if I leave you alone, / [you will not live]" is found also in the Bible: "Do not withhold discipline from your children; / if you beat them with a rod, / they will not die. / If you beat them with the rod, / you will save their lives from Sheol" (Prov 23:13-14).

3. THE BOOK OF PROVERBS

1. See chap. 2, n. 3.

2. Helmut Brunner, *Die Weisheitsbücher der Ägypter* (2nd ed.; Munich: Artemis, 1991). Ten of the instructions have been translated into English in *AEL,* and several are represented in *ANET.*

3. See the discussion of the instruction in chapter 2.

4. A fine analysis of the problem is M. V. Fox, "The Social Location of the Book of Proverbs," in Fox et al., *Texts, Temples, and Traditions: A Tribute to Menahem Haran* (Winona Lake, Ind.: Eisenbrauns, 1996), 227-39.

5. Fox, "The Social Location," 239.

6. Samuel Johnson, *Rambler,* no. 2, cited in W. J. Bate, *Samuel Johnson* (New York: Harcourt Brace Jovanovich, 1977), 291.

7. Samuel Johnson, essay on Alexander Pope, in *Lives of the English Poets.*

8. *Proverbios* Nueva biblia Española (Madrid: Ediciones Cristiandad, 1984), 256 among other places.

9. Metonymy is "a figure in which one word is substituted for another on the basis of some material, causal, or conceptual relation," e.g., container for thing contained, agent for act, product, or object possessed, cause for effect, etc. (Alex Preminger and T. V. F. Brogan, *The New Princeton Encyclopedia of Poetry and Poetics* [Princeton: Princeton University, 1993], 783).

10. "Son" can designate the real son of the teacher or a student. "Child" is not a satisfactory English translation, for it implies one who is unable to make a life decision. "Disciple" is a better, though not perfect, translation.

11. For a detailed study of Proverbs' vocabulary of wisdom, see M. Fox, "Words for Wisdom," *Zeitschrift für Althebraistik* 6 (1993): 149-65.

12. For "way," see N. Habel, "The Symbolism of Wisdom in Proverbs 1–9," *Interpretation* 26 (1972): 131-57, and R. C. Van Leeuwen, "Liminality

and Worldview in Proverbs 1–9," *Semeia* 50 (1990): 111-44. For the metaphor of walk as self-conduct in living, see F. J. Helfmeyer, "*Hālakh,*" in G. J. Botterweck and H. Ringgren, *Theological Dictionary of the Old Testament,* vol. 3 (Grand Rapids: Eerdmans, 1978), 388-403.

13. Jutta Hausmann, *Studien zum Menschenbild der älteren Weisheit (Spr 10ff.)* Forschungen zum Alten Testament 7 (Tübingen: Mohr [Siebeck], 1995), 342.

14. The word occurs forty-two times in Proverbs, many more times if we count its many synonyms. The concern holds good for other biblical wisdom books: eighteen times in Job, twenty-eight times in Qoheleth, sixty times (Greek *sophia*) in Sirach, and thirty times in the Wisdom of Solomon.

15. For the evidence that Woman Wisdom is a literary construct and foil to Folly, see R. Clifford, "Woman Wisdom in the Book of Proverbs," in G. Braulik et al., *Biblische Theologie und gesellschaftlicher Wandel* Lohfink volume (Freiburg: Herder, 1993), 61-72.

16. For the notion of systematic metaphors such as argument as war or time as money, see George Lakoff and Mark Johnson, *Metaphors We Live By* (Chicago: University of Chicago, 1980).

17. Several recent studies have cast important light on the translation and structure of this chapter: Roland Murphy, "Wisdom's Song: Proverbs 1:20-33," *CBQ* 48 (1986): 456-60; Maurice Gilbert, "Le discours menaçant de Sagesse en Proverbes 1,20-33," in D. Garrone and F. Israel, eds., *Storia e Tradizioni di Israele* Soggin vol. (Brescia: Paideia, 1991), 99-119.

18. There is a considerable body of scholarly writing on rich and poor in Proverbs. See R. N. Whybray, *Wealth and Poverty in the Book of Proverbs* JSOTSup 99 (Sheffield: JSOT, 1990).

19. No. 7, my translation of Brunner, *Die Weisheitsbücher der Ägypter,* 114 (his italics).

4. THE BOOK OF JOB

1. From the Middle Kingdom onward, the *ba* was an existence-form of a dead Egyptian, a principle of vitality.

2. *ANET,* 589-91, and *TUAT,* vol. 3, pp. 102-9. Though the manuscripts are of the second millennium, the original composition was probably in the third.

3. Translations that include the more complete text of tablet I include *BM,* vol. 1, pp. 308-21, and *TUAT,* vol. 3, pp. 110-35. A fragmentary Akkadian text, related in theme to *Ludlul,* was found in Ugarit. It is to be dated to before 1200 B.C.E. See *BM,* vol. 1, pp. 326-27, and *TUAT,* vol. 3, pp. 140-43.

4. W. L. Moran, "Notes on the Hymn to Marduk in *Ludlul bēl nēmeqi,*" *Journal of the American Oriental Society* 103 (1983): 253-60, and an address given at August 1992 meeting of the Catholic Biblical Association in Washington, D.C.

5. The text and translation is in Lambert, *BWL,* 63-91. Translations are in *BM,* vol. 2, pp. 806-14; *TUAT,* vol. 3., pp. 143-58.

6. W. L. Moran, "Rib Adda: Job at Byblos?" in *Biblical and Related Studies Presented to Samuel Iwry* (Winona Lake: Eisenbrauns, 1985), 176-77.

7. Ibid., 177 n. 16.

8. The famous phrase in James 5:10, the "patience *(hypomonē)* of Job," is better translated "endurance" in trials, and can be applied to Job throughout the book, not just in the prologue and epilogue.

9. H. Habel, *The Book of Job* (London: S.C.M., 1985), 102.

10. My remarks draw on Habel's analysis.

11. Michael Fishbane calls this revision "aggadic exegesis," *Biblical Interpretation in Ancient Israel* (Oxford: Clarendon, 1985), 285.

12. Habel, *Book of Job*, 205.

13. See P. W. Skehan, "Strophic Patterns in the Book of Job," *CBQ* 23 (1961): 141. The possibility is entertained by M. Greenberg, "Job," in R. Alter and F. Kermode, eds., *The Literary Guide to the Bible* (Cambridge, Mass.: Harvard University, 1987), 293-94, and J. G. Janzen, *Job* Interpretation (Atlanta: John Knox, 1985).

14. Habel, *Book of Job,* 388-401.

15. Ibid., 427-31.

16. I read *ya ' ăne,* "he will respond," for MT *yĕ ' anneh,* "he will afflict," with Habel, *Book of Job,* for (1) Elihu had previously taken a positive view of divine affliction *('onî)* in 38:6 and 15; (2) "he will not respond" balances the opening of v. 23, "we cannot find him." Verse 24 plays on the similar Hebrew verbs "fear" *yĕrē'û* and "see" *yir'eh.*

17. *Book of Job,* 517-74. For the divine speeches, I draw on my analysis published in *Creation Accounts in the Ancient Near East and in the Bible* CBQMS 26 (Washington, D.C.: Catholic Biblical Association, 1994), 190-97.

18. Hebrew *'ēṣâ* ("design") occurs in Job nine times. Apart from the speeches of God in chapters 38–41, six times it means "plan," usually the plan of the wicked that God seemingly allows to prosper (5:13; 10:3; 12:13; 18:7; 21:16; 22:18). God's first reply to Job picks up this word, which implies arbitrary and capricious rule.

19. The remainder of this section is drawn largely from my *Creation Accounts,* 191-97. The outline is found in Habel, *Book of Job,* 526-27.

20. Hebrew *rōb* is a participle of *rîb,* "to bring suit, complain." So Habel, *Book of Job,* see under 40:2.

21. The Similitudes of Enoch are usually dated to the last half of the first century B.C. or the first three quarters of the first century A.D., but they contain old mythology. For solid arguments against taking the creatures merely as natural animals, see M. Pope, *Job* Anchor Bible 15, 3rd ed. (Garden City, N.Y.: Doubleday, 1973), 320-23.

22. The preceding Hebrew verse is overlong and 40:24*a* is too short, leading many scholars to one of two emendations: to add *mî hû'* ("Who is there who") to the beginning of v. 24*a,* or to attach the last two words of v. 23*b* to v. 24*a.* In the latter solution, they revocalize *'el pîhû* as *'ēl* ("God"). In any case, the Hebrew text correctly understands the subject to be God.

23. J. D. Levenson, *Creation and the Persistence of Evil: The Jewish Drama of Divine Omnipotence* (San Francisco: Harper & Row, 1988), 49.

24. Greenberg, "Job," 298.

25. And just as he did, we might add, of Behemoth. There is a certain parallel between the two troubling beings, both of whom belong to God's universe.

5. THE BOOK OF QOHELETH (ECCLESIASTES)

1. Gilgamesh was a historical king of the third millennium about whom adventure tales, written in Sumerian, were told within a few decades of his death. In the Old Babylonian period (ca. 1950–1530 B.C.E.), the stories were woven into a long epic, in which Gilgamesh and his friend Enkidu attempt to conquer death. The standard version developed from the Old Babylonian version.

2. Trans. E. A. Speiser, *ANET*, 90.

3. *MFM*, 50-51. For a general view, see W. L. Moran, "Gilgamesh," in *Encyclopedia of Religion*, ed. M. Eliade, vol. 5 (New York: Macmillan, 1981), 557-60: "In contrast to the hymn with which the [Old Babylonian] epic once began—a celebration of Gilgamesh's physical power and noble origins— the new lines [among them, the first forty lines of the prologue] emphasize not his strength but the range of his experience and knowledge, and the sufferings they cost him. By a tissue of allusions to a genre of pseudo-auto-biography in which kings made lessons of their lives and recorded them for posterity, these lines also imply that Gilgamesh did the same. Based on and authenticated by this source, the epic, now addressing a reader ("thou") and intending to instruct him, becomes a part of wisdom litera-ture" (559).

4. For the linguistic evidence, see C. L. Seow, *Ecclesiastes* Anchor Bible 18C (New York: Doubleday, 1997), esp. 20-21. J. Kugel uses similar linguis-tic and economic grounds, as well as other reasons, to arrive at nearly the same date, "Qoheleth and Money," *CBQ* 51 (1989): 46-49.

5. Kugel, "Qoheleth and Money," 46.

6. Seow, *Ecclesiastes*, 21-32.

7. Ibid., 23.

8. A. G. Wright, "Ecclesiastes (Qoheleth)" in *NJBC*, 489 (abridged).

9. N. Lohfink, *Kohelet* Neue Echter Bibel. (Würzburg: Echter Verlag, 1980), 10.

10. Hebrew *dābār* can be "word" or "thing."

11. See Seow, *Ecclesiastes*, 144-45, and "Qohelet's Autobiography," in *Fortunate the Eyes That See* (D. N. Freedman volume); ed. A. Beck et al. (Grand Rapids, Mich.: Eerdmans, 1995), 257-82. Some of the relevant royal inscriptions can be found in *ANET*, 653-56.

12. A commentator who has underscored the importance of death in Qoheleth is Lohfink, "Man Face to Face with Death," in *The Christian Meaning of the Old Testament* (Milwaukee: Bruce, 1968), 138-69, and "The Present and Eternity: Time in Qoheleth," *Theology Digest* 34 (1987): 236-40.

13. See Seow, *Ecclesiastes*, for discussion. MT *aḥărê*, "after," is to be read *aḥărāy*, "after me," and *hammelek*, "the king" is to be read *hămōlēk*, "shall he control?"

14. D. C. Fredericks, "Chiasm and Parallel Structure in Qoheleth 5:6– 6:9," *JBL* 108 (1989): 26-38. I quote Seow's adaptation, *Ecclesiastes*, 217.

15. The NRSV makes the subject plural in vv. 12-16 (EV 13-17), which obscures the parallel with 6:3-6.

16. So Seow, *Ecclesiastes*, 274, who points out that *'ādām* elsewhere in Qoheleth always means "human being" not "male" as here.

17. So Wright, *Ecclesiastes* in *NJBC;* Seow, *Ecclesiastes;* Murphy, *Ecclesiastes* Word Biblical Commentary 23A (Dallas: Word, 1992); and Lohfink, *Kohelet.* Wright and Murphy treat 11:8–12:8 separately, and Lohfink begins the section at 9:7.

18. The expression of an idea with two independent words joined by "and," for example, "nice and warm" for "nicely warm."

19. The latter interpretation is like the admonition found in the Jerusalem Talmud, "Everyone must give an account before God of all good things one saw in life and did not enjoy" (*Qiddušin* 4:12, quoted in Seow, *Ecclesiastes,* 371).

20. The plural is either the "plural of majesty" or an instance of the common confusion in late Hebrew between III-alep and III-Weak roots.

21. Vivid descriptions of the onslaughts of old age are found in Egyptian literature: *The Instructions of Ptahhotep,* 1.3-10 (*AEL,* vol. 1, pp. 62-63); *The Tale of Sinuhe,* lines 167-70 (*AEL,* vol. 1, p. 229); *The Instruction of Papyrus Insinger* 17.11-14 (*AEL,* vol. 3, p. 199). All are cited by Seow, *Ecclesiastes,* 372-75.

22. M. Fox, *Qoheleth and His Contradictions* (Sheffield: Almond, 1989), 85-106.

23. Walther Zimmerli, *Sprüche, Prediger* Altes Testament Deutsch 16/1 (Göttingen: Vandenhoeck & Ruprecht, 1963).

24. J. L. Crenshaw, *Ecclesiastes* Old Testament Library (Philadelphia: Westminster, 1987).

25. Lohfink, *Kohelet,* 15.

26. Murphy, *Ecclesiastes,* lvi-lxix.

27. Ibid., lxix, quoting Hertzberg, *Der Prediger* Kommentar zum Alten Testament 17/4 (Gütersloh: Mohn, 1963), 237-38.

28. Dietrich Bonhoeffer, *Letters and Papers from Prison* (New York: Macmillan, 1971), 157.

29. Fox, *Qoheleth and His Contradictions,* 10-12.

6. THE WISDOM OF BEN SIRA (SIRACH)

1. Sir 50:1-4 presupposes Simon's death, an event that took place ca. 196 B.C.E.

2. R. Pautrel, "Ben Sira et le Stoïcisme," *Recherches de science religieuse* 51 (1963): 534-49, cited in A. Minissale, *Siracide* (Rome: Edizioni Paoline, 1980), 16.

3. Minissale, *Siracide,* 16.

4. Ibid., p. 9; P. W. Skehan and A. A. Di Lella, *The Wisdom of Ben Sira* Anchor Bible 39 (New York: Doubleday, 1989), xiii-xvi.

5. In antiquity—and this is especially clear in Mesopotamian texts—the world was a given, simply there. There were many expressions for the cosmic arrangement, among them Akkadian *šimtu* and Sumerian *namtar, me,* and *gišhur.* In Egypt, the same basic idea was expressed by *maat.*

6. In Greek, the negative particle *ou* (= Hebrew *lō* is the first word in v. 22, which suggests that in the original Hebrew *l,* the twelfth letter, began

the second part of the poem. "V. 21" is judged by commentators to be "Greek II" and thus not part of the original text.

7. "Merism reduces a complete series to two of its constituent elements, or it divides a whole into two halves. 'Mountains and valleys' represent the whole countryside" (L. Alonso Schökel, *A Manual of Hebrew Poetics* [Rome: Pontifical Biblical Institute, 1988], 83).

8. M. Gilbert, "Siracide," in *Dictionnaire de la Bible. Supplément,* vol. 12 (Paris: Letouzey & Ané, 1996), col. 1427.

9. See R. Clifford, "The Hebrew Scriptures and the Theology of Creation," *Theological Studies* 46 (1985): 507-23, and *Creation Accounts in the Ancient Near East and in the Bible* CBQMS 25 (Washington, D.C.: Catholic Biblical Association, 1994).

10. Gilbert, "Siracide," col. 1422. See the following studies on the Praise of the Wise Ancestors (or Praise of the Fathers): B. L. Mack, *Wisdom and the Hebrew Epic: Ben Sira's Hymn of Praise of the Fathers* (Chicago: University of Chicago, 1985); T. R. Lee, *Studies in the Form of Sirach 440-50* SBLDS 75 (Atlanta, Ga.; Scholars Press, 1986); J. D. Martin, "Ben Sira's Hymn to the Fathers: A Messianic Perspective," *Old Testament Studies* 24 (1986): 107-23; P. C. Beentjes, "The 'Praise of the Famous' and Its Prologue: Some Observations on Ben Sira 44:1-15 and the Question of Enoch in 44:16," *Bijdragen Tijdschrift voor Filosofie e Theologie* 45 (1984): 373-84.

11. 44:17, 18 *(b'wt),* 20, 22; 45:15, 24, 25.

12. R. Hayward, "Sacrifice and World Order: Some Observations on Ben Sira's Attitude to the Temple Service," in S. W. Sykes, ed., *Sacrifice and Redemption: Durham Essays in Theology* (Cambridge: Cambridge University, 1991), 22-34.

13. Trans. Skehan and Di Lella, *The Wisdom of Ben Sira,* 329. They do not regard v. 34 as authentic here, "Notice that I have not labored for myself alone, / but for all who seek wisdom."

14. So J. Haspecker, *Gottesfurcht bei Jesus Sirach: Ihre religiöse Struktur und ihre literarische und doctrinäre Bedeutung* Analecta Biblica 30 (Rome: Pontifical Biblical Institute, 1967).

15. G. von Rad, *Wisdom in Israel* (Nashville/New York: Abingdon Press, 1972), 242; and J. Marbock, *Weisheit im Wandel: Untersuchungen zur Weisheitstheologie bei Ben Sira* Bonner biblische Beiträge 37 (Bonn: Hanstein, 1971).

16. This view is similar to chap. 10 in the Wisdom of Solomon, except that Ben Sira does not hesitate to criticize individual Israelites.

17. This is G. Prato's own summary of his *Il problema della teodicea in Ben Sira* Analecta Biblica 65 (Rome: Pontifical Biblical Institute, 1975), cited by Gilbert, "Siracide," col. 1434.

18. The topic of women in Sirach is more subtle than might appear at first reading and repays study. See H. McKeating, "Jesus Ben Sira's Attitude to Women," *Expository Times* 85 (1973-74): 85-87; M. Gilbert, "Ben Sira et la femme," *Revue théologique de Louvain* 7 (1976): 426-42; C. Camp, "Understanding Patriarchy: Women in Second-Century Jerusalem Through the Eyes of Ben Sira," in A. J. Levine, ed., *Women Like This: New Perspectives on Jewish Women in the Greco-Roman World* (Atlanta, Ga.: Scholars Press, 1991), 1-39.

7. THE WISDOM OF SOLOMON

1. Septuagint means "seventy"; its abbreviation is LXX. The number seventy-two was rounded off to seventy.

2. A good introduction to Hellenistic culture is a biography of Alexander, such as Peter Green, *Alexander the Great* (New York: Praeger, 1970) or a general survey such as Frank W. Walbank, *The Hellenistic World*, rev. ed. (Cambridge: Harvard, 1993).

3. M. Gilbert, from whose magisterial survey I draw heavily, also begins with the literary structure rather than with the genre, "Sagesse de Salomon (ou Livre de la Sagesse)," *Dictionnaire de la Bible. Supplément*, vol. 12 (Paris: Letouzey & Ané, 1996), cols. 58-119.

4. Our outline owes much to A. A. Wright, "The Structure of the Book of Wisdom," *Biblica* 48 (1967): 165-84; James M. Reese, *Hellenistic Influence on the Book of Wisdom and Its Consequences* Analecta Biblica 41 (Rome: Biblical Institute, 1970); M. Gilbert, *La critique des dieux dans le Livre de la Sagesse (Sg 13-15)* Analecta Biblica 53 (Rome: Biblical Institute, 1973), and esp. his "Sagesse de Salomon."

5. The italicized type refers to the Egyptian experience, the roman type to the Israelites'.

6. Reese, *Hellenistic Influence on the Book of Wisdom*. He has been followed by D. Winston, *The Wisdom of Solomon* Anchor Bible 43 (Garden City, N.Y.: Doubleday, 1979), 18-20.

7. Gilbert, "Sagesse de Salomon," cols. 86-87.

8. This treatment owes much to D. Georgi, "Der vorpaulinische Hymnus Phil 2, s6-11," *Zeit und Geschichte* R. Bultmann vol.; ed. E. Kinkler (Tübingen: J. C. B. Mohr, 1964), 262-93.

9. "Mysteries" is used in the same sense in the New Testament.

10. The NRSV unfortunately translates the singulars as plurals here, obscuring the reference to Enoch as a type.

11. For the theme of creation, see M. Kolarcik, "Creation and Salvation in the Book of Wisdom," in R. Clifford and J. J. Collins, eds., *Creation in the Biblical Traditions* CBQMS 24 (Washington, D.C.; Catholic Biblical Association, 1992), 97-107.

12. See G. W. Nickelsburg, *Resurrection, Immortality, and Eternal Life in Intertestamental Judaism* HTS 26 (Cambridge, Mass.: Harvard, 1972), 48-92.

13. Winston, *Wisdom of Solomon*, 184.

14. The definition is that of G. H. Box and Oesterley (1911), quoted with approval by Winston, *Wisdom of Solomon*, 34.

15. Gilbert, "Sagesse de Salomon," col. 108.

8. THE SONG OF SONGS

1. Michael Fox, *The Song of Songs and the Ancient Egyptian Love Songs* (Madison: University of Wisconsin, 1985), 181-93.

2. Ibid., 247.

3. Ibid., 250-52.

4. Fox, *Song of Songs,* 3-81. Fox is much more complete than the selections in *AEL,* vol. 2, pp. 181-93, and in W. K. Simpson, *The Literature of Ancient Egypt* (New Haven, Conn.: Yale University, 1972), 297-306.

5. Fox, *Song of Songs,* 23.

6. Ibid., 52 (excerpt).

7. The following approach is indebted to Fox, 209-26.

8. The following comments owe much to M. Falk, *The Song of Songs: A New Translation and Interpretation* (San Francisco: Harper, 1990), 113-23.

9. Ibid., 139-42.

10. Ibid., 143-50.

9. WISDOM IN JUDAISM AND CHRISTIANITY

1. B. Witherington III, *Jesus the Sage: The Pilgrimage of Wisdom* (Minneapolis: Fortress, 1994).

2. A fine study of the available texts is D. J. Harrington, *Wisdom Texts from Qumran* (New York: Routledge, 1996).

3. The following remarks owe much to R. Brown, *The Gospel According to John,* vol. 1, Anchor Bible 29 (Garden City, N.Y.: Doubleday, 1966), cxii-cxv.

INDEX OF TOPICS

INDEX OF AUTHORS

INDEX OF AUTHORS